Diabetes at 14

Flower Press

DIABETES at 14:

Choosing Tighter Control
for an
Active Life

by

William G. Melluish
with illustrations by Paul M. Bourgeois

Flower Press
Kalamazoo, Michigan USA

Diabetes at 14: Choosing Tighter Control for an Active Life, by William G. Melluish.

Publisher's Cataloging-in-Publication
(Provided by Quality Books, Inc.)

Melluish, William G.
    Diabetes at 14 : choosing tighter control for an active life / by William G. Melluish ; with illustrations by Paul M. Bourgeois. — 1st ed.
        p. cm.
    Includes bibliographical references and index.
    SUMMARY: A college athlete and musician who was diagnosed with insulin-dependent diabetes as a teenager explains how other teens can learn to control the disease.
    ISBN: 0-942256-12-3

    1. Melluish, William G.—Health—Juvenile literature. 2. Diabetics—United States—Biography—Juvenile literature. 3. Diabetes in adolescence—Juvenile literature. 4. Diabetes—Treatment—Juvenile literature.   I. Title.

RC660.5.M45 2000   362.1'9892462
                                     QB199-1473

Flower Press
10332 Shaver Road
Kalamazoo, MI 49024

Table of Contents

Preface, with a note on diabetes vii

Introduction, with a note to parents xvii

Chapter 1. What's wrong with me? 1
            Critical substances 4
            Weights and measures 6

Chapter 2. Life begins to change for me 9
            Body fluid testing............................ 14
            Substance tests 17
            Insulin injections 20

Chapter 3. That first hypoglycemic episode 23
            Hypoglycemia 27
            Metabolism and stress 31

Chapter 4. Learning to plan ahead 33
            Diabetic supply sources 36
            Snacks... 37
            Carbohydrate loading 39

Chapter 5. School adjustments 43
            School policies 46
            Injection sites 49

Chapter 6. Freedom lost 51
            Insulins... 54
            Diet 56
            Food biochemistry............................ 58

Chapter 7. Freedom found 61
            Complications and risk
                reduction.............................. 67
            Insulin timing 71

Chapter 8. Athletics..................................... 75
            Complex carbohydrates 79
            Food exchanges 80
            Exercise and stress 82

Chapter 9. A handy new tool..................... 85
            Pre-meal tests 89

Chapter 10. Fine tuning for the long haul 93
            Injection-site rotation 97

Chapter 11. Finer tuning............................ 99
            FDA 106

Chapter 12. A visit to my doctor 109

Chapter 13. Getting on with my life 117

Afterword 121
            Word construction 121
            More on critical substances........... 122
            Body fluid testing 124
            Blood 126
            Urine.............................. 134
            Insulins.............................. 138
            Support organizations 139

Reading 141

Index 147

About the author 167

Preface

Allow me to introduce myself as Bill
Melluish. This is a story about my struggles with
diabetes as a teenager. I am not a medical doctor,
nurse, dietitian, or diabetes educator. I am a young
adult who got a disease and did not want it to
hinder my life. This book will show you, as an
insulin-dependent diabetic who is also a young
adult, that diabetes does not have to hold you
back. It should convey the idea that it is possible
to get good control of your blood sugar and to
lead a life that is not controlled by a disease.

When I was diagnosed with Type I diabetes, chaos took over my life, as it first does to
anyone with diabetes. The new schedules, a new
diet, new knowledge, and a new way of life, were
all changes for me. No one else could relate to
them. During my first trips to the doctor's office,

a few books were recommended to me, but after looking into them, I found that none both told a story and gave information that I, as an active teenager, was looking for. I really wished there had been a book out there for me. With the added confusion in my life and the lack of confidence I had with my newly diagnosed disease, I never thought that I would be the one to write it.

After the original commotion, the early days of living with my diabetes proved to be quite normal. There was a period of fine tuning for normal activities and special events—then times when new situations would arise. As an athlete, I noticed that this usually happened with the passing of the seasons. My life-style with its many variables kept changing as time marched on, but my blood sugar readings stayed pretty much the same. I did have an occasional high or low, but I recovered immediately.

So there I was, taking more and more steps towards "freedom" from my disease, as my readings were staying consistently good. My doctors were commending me for taking such good care of myself, but I did not think much of it—I merely thought I was living my life like anyone else.

When my mom heard how good my trips to the doctor had been, she began to think that my knowledge and experience could be very beneficial to other kids my age who are going through the same changes. She suggested writing a book, but I never actually thought it would happen. I was only 16 years old. Did I have much to offer others who knew they had diabetes, perhaps for more than the two years since my own diagnosis? My mom kept bringing up her idea; I kept putting it off.

When I was 17 years old, counseling at a camp for kids with diabetes ignited my desire to help them. I saw hundreds of kids who could not control their blood sugar and had little freedom in their lives. They had parents who understood their child's disease better than their child did. Campers would not give blood sugar readings in the 300's another thought. This bothered me a great deal. In many kids, I saw a troublesome offhand attitude towards a serious disease. I could see it probably turning into very casual life-styles, presenting problems and complications, that would restrict them in the future.

Upon returning home from camp, I discussed these worries with my parents. They were as surprised as I had been. In addition to her amazement, my mom decided that I was going to write this book whether I wanted to or not. My doctor even thought it would be a great thing to do and, when he agreed to edit and correct any of the medical specifics, I started writing. After each chapter, my dad reviewed what I had written.

The whole process was challenging because I had forgotten how much I had learned throughout my education about the disease. It was difficult, and even scary, to go back and remember what it was like when I had first heard the words,

"You have diabetes." So much needed to be learned, and that hasn't changed.

Each chapter in this book tries to explain what I have gone through in regulating my disease. Mine is a story with which you, no doubt, will be able to relate. I hope my story will give you a better understanding and management of this complicated disease we have in common. Closing most chapters, "Notes" provide general "how to" information for those newly diagnosed with diabetes. More details of the "when, where, who, what, and why" about diabetes and its effects in our bodies are found in a back matter section, "Afterword." These details may be helpful to and promote deeper understanding in those who have lived with diabetes awhile.

A Note on Diabetes

Diabetes is a chronic disorder of an endocrine gland that secretes hormones directly into the bloodstream. The word *diabetes* itself refers to the production and passing of abnormally large amounts of urine. An impaired pituitary leads to diabetes insipidus and an impaired pancreas leads to diabetes mellitus. Excessive thirst is a symptom for either disease.

Normally a healthy person might drink up to 8-10 glasses of water every day and get up during the night once or twice to go to the bathroom. Passing more than two quarts of urine in a 24-hour period, however, is typical for someone with diabetes. Sometimes doctors use vague descriptions like "abnormally large" and "excessive." Even people with a family history of diabetes—those who have an idea of what their relatives may have experienced—often procrastinate in making a doctor's appointment because they don't want to know what might be wrong. The worst case, however, is quite manageable.

Two types of diabetes mellitus or "sugar diabetes" occur. For every child or young adult who contracts Type I insulin-dependent diabetes mellitus, nine older people develop less severe Type II non-insulin-dependent diabetes mellitus. Health care professionals are worried about how many more Type II cases are showing up in elementary school children. The Centers for Disease Control and Prevention (CDC), a federal public health agency in Atlanta, notes that Type II is increasing by 6% per year in adolescents.

Approximately 500,000 students have diabetes, with estimates ranging from 1 in 300 to 1 in 600 of the school-age population (kindergarten through high school). Diabetics comprise 6.6% of the U.S. population, including 22,500 teenagers in grades 9-12 and 13,000 new cases in children every year. Eight million take insulin, but more than one-third of treated diabetics are uncontrolled on their regimens. Diabetes is estimated to cost our health care systems at least $100 billion per year.

People with Type I diabetes mellitus, a disease known for 4,000 years, have an impaired pancreas that cannot make insulin. Controlling its symptoms became possible only in the 1920s when two Canadians shared a Nobel Prize for using insulin extracts from pancreatic tissue to demonstrate their effect on blood sugar levels. Sculpted images of Sir Frederick Banting and his associate are among the parade of figures illustrating the history of medicine on the façade of the research-oriented Joslin Diabetes Center in Boston.

People are not alone in living with diabetes mellitus. Some dogs and cats also have an impaired pancreas that is unable to produce enough of the hormone to meet their energy-producing needs. In fact, insulin was first discovered in dogs.

Many people besides my parents have helped put this book together. My doctor, Martin B. Draznin, specializes in endocrinology and diabetology, and very carefully reviewed a late draft. Several nurses and diabetes educators also did the same: Rebecca Emerson, RN, BSN, CDE, who has worked with me for at least five years; Michele

Heckman, MSN, RN, CDE, CS; and, Marie Stoline, RN. I have also received letters of support and encouraging comments from other diabetics, including guys my age who were diagnosed with Type I diabetes as children or teenagers and their parents: Ms. Sandi Shaw, Trent Frisch, Philip Jordon, Dallas Shannon, Lois Kamoi, and Mrs. Joanne Frisch. We all believe this book will become a reference guide to keeping a Type I condition in perspective.

Once again, I am not a medical doctor. I only share with you my experience of coping successfully because it has worked for me. More importantly, I hope it will also help you reclaim more of your former pre-diagnosis freedom for your already complicated life right now.

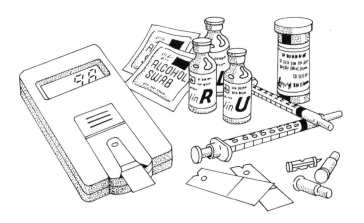

Introduction

All summer long I watched my fourteen year old son Bill grow taller and not gain any weight even though he was eating like a horse. I am a doctor who specializes in eye disease. However, I know a lot of general medicine, and became

worried that there may have been something wrong with Bill's health. In August I dropped him off at Van Buren Summer Youth Camp for a week of being a camp counselor trainee.

As Bill walked away, he appeared slimmer than I had ever seen him. It really frightened me enough so that I resolved then and there to have his orthopedic surgeon, who was to operate on his old shoulder injury in two weeks, give him a thorough check-up before the surgery. His exam was very complete. Bill's blood count and urinalysis were normal, but the worry was still grinding at me. My suspicions later proved to be well-based.

A Note to Parents

When Bill first got diabetes, it was emotionally tough on me because I practice ophthalmology and daily take care of people whose vision is affected by diabetes. Knowing that good glucose control is the key to staying healthy for patients with diabetes, and hoping that Bill would learn to do this well, I became very attentive to the reasons why my patients either became, or never became, good managers of their diabetes.

It quickly became clear to me that there are several causes behind becoming a poor diabetes manager:

1. *A fatalistic approach to complications*—assumes there is nothing one can do to avoid the long-term complications of diabetes.

2. *Ignorance and denial*—allows well-meaning parents, care givers, or patients themselves to feel safe doing little or nothing about problems looming on the horizon due to poor control.

3. *Doctors*—foster needless dependence when they do not keep abreast of new knowledge and technology or choose not to share with their patients what they do learn. New and better management regimens require extra work, some trial and error, and frustration for both patients and the doctors themselves.

4. *Low expectations of diabetic control*—lead new patients to give up before they even try, unfortunately reinforced by their parents or their doctors.

Bill has done well with his disease because his mother and I gave him all the important knowledge and help then available. We did not keep him ignorant, nor allow him to adopt a fatalistic approach. Most importantly, however, he had, and still has, a doctor and diabetes care team that are top notch and dedicated to helping teens with diabetes prepare for a relatively normal life. By giving them knowledge, confidence, up-to-date care, and high expectations, this team focuses on building lives that are healthy, independent, and minimally restricted.

I sincerely hope you can find this kind of support for your child, but the rest of the story is Bill's, and he tells it best because he lived it.

James W. Melluish, MD

Chapter 1

What's Wrong with Me?

I am the youngest of six children. We live in a medium-sized town in Michigan and the last of my siblings had just left home for college when the story begins.

As a result of multiple injuries to my right shoulder from skiing, snowboarding, and playing basketball, I had it surgically repaired at summer's

1

end in 1993, two days before I was to begin high school. My blood count and urinalysis, done at the hospital as part of my procedure, were normal. After the successful surgery, I awoke with a lot of pain in my shoulder and a lot of nausea from the anesthetic. I also awoke with a fatigue that would strangely continue for a long time.

As my rehabilitation from surgery progressed over time, my shoulder became significantly stronger. I got back its full range of motion, but I still felt very fatigued. While my shoulder was in a sling and demanded my attention, I assumed my lack of energy was due to not being able to exercise much.

Besides the fatigue, I started becoming very thirsty and urinating very frequently. I would wake up two or three times during the night to go to the bathroom. I still thought that the thirst and fatigue were due to a lack of exercise, plus lack of perspiring. About three weeks after surgery, I was urinating almost every hour, losing a large volume every time. Then my vision began to blur—I really had to concentrate to see clearly. After talking with my father, who is a medical doctor specializing in eye diseases, we agreed to look for objective help from outside my family.

Approximately two weeks earlier in mid-September, I had just had a general physical at my doctor's office. He had no reason to order another urinalysis so soon after my pre-surgery check-up because I had not told him about my urinating problem. I really did not think much about it.

For a subsequent post-op visit on the morning of September 27th, however, my pediatrician Dr. Arthur Feinberg had me bring a urine sample into his office. He found *sugar* and *ketones* in it. His call to my mother and me had some sense of urgency, asking us to visit him that afternoon. Dr. Feinberg had also had my blood sugar tested—it was 291 mg/dl, which is about three times higher than normal!

NOTES

CRITICAL SUBSTANCES

Sugars

Different forms of sugar are produced by both plants and animals. Sucrose is part of both molasses and table sugar, derived from sugar cane and sugar beets. Other plant sugars include gulose in syrups, fructose in fruits, and galactose in binding and thickening agents. Animal-produced sugars are lactose in milk and fructose in honey and semen. Although simple glucose occurs in most plant and animal tissues, in our bodies it usually comes from digesting other kinds of sugars, then circulates in our blood as the major energy source.

Blood Sugar

What is sugar doing in our blood? Some glucose in the blood is normal, regardless if a person has diabetes or not. A major purpose of blood is to carry substances from place to place inside our bodies. Blood carries sugar to cells. Body cells can store sugar in a more complex form or release the energy in it for constructive types of work— repairing injuries, fighting infections, making new cells—or just staying alive.

Blood sugar levels depend on a combination of at least four factors: food, insulin, exercise, and stress. In actuality how your body processes the food you eat, activating many hormones not limited to but certainly including insulin, is quite complicated. Its goal is to produce enough energy to respond to a variety of stimuli, including exercise and stress, without overloading the glucose load to your kidneys.

"Everything in moderation" means that too much of anything probably causes trouble. So it is with blood sugar.

Too much disrupts normal functioning, just as disease conditions do. High blood sugar rarely occurs in healthy non-diabetics, except in glucose tolerance tests; temporary headache and nausea are typical results. In people with diabetes, however, its consequences are more severe.

Ketones

We're not talking about pianos or vocal groups here. Ketones are substances containing the chemical elements carbon and oxygen whose atoms are double-bonded together with the carbon usually attached to other groups. Within the sugar called fructose is a carbonyl group, attached to two carbon atoms, which identifies it as a ketone. The simplest ketone, however, is acetone, which evaporates easily and is highly flammable.

When proteins and stored fat inside our bodies begin to be used abnormally for energy, *ketone bodies* (acids) slowly build up first in the blood. Then they spill over into the urine. It takes four hours of ketones in the urine, or *ketonuria*, before acidosis occurs. During metabolic acidosis, nitrogen atoms in protein molecules reconfigure themselves to promptly release hydrogen ions (H^+). This makes the urine's pH dip below 4.8 becoming more acid. In *diabetic ketoacidosis*, getting rid of such acids is the body's high priority.

Acetone, taking excretory paths through the kidneys and the lungs, gives both urine and exhaled breath a fruity odor. Other symptoms of diabetic ketoacidosis include deep and rapid breathing, rapid and weak pulse, low blood pressure, dehydration, and excretion of very large amounts of ammonium ion (NH_4^+). They broadcast severe, out-of-control diabetes (high blood sugar) that needs emergency treatment right away. Ignoring ketonuria may result first in acidosis, then coma with possible brain swelling. Immediate treatment to prevent coma, and even death, involves administration of fluids and insulin, and perhaps hospitalization that costs thousands of dollars. Prevention of acidosis means maintaining insulin levels appropriate to activity.

WEIGHTS AND MEASURES

Blood sugar levels are reported as mg/dl (milligrams per deciliter), the weight of glucose in a specific volume of blood. Mass and volume in different measurement systems carry particular labels. Science and its branches, like biology, chemistry, and medicine throughout the world, use metric system labels, such as milligrams, grams, deciliters, and liters. In the U.S., however, we commonly use the English system of ounces and pounds to describe how much a mass weighs, and pints and quarts for amounts of liquid volume.

The table on the following page contains a summary of the unit names, abbreviations, and conversion quantities of all weights and measures mentioned in this book.

Selected Weights and Measures

Label Abbreviation	Measure	Conversion Quantities
cc	cubic centimeter	100 units of insulin or 1 ml or 0.033 oz
dl	deciliter	one-tenth of a liter or 0.10 liter or 3.38 fl oz
g	gram	metric unit of mass and weight or 0.035 oz
gal	gallon	3.78 liters or 4 qt
kg	kilogram	1000 g or 2.2 lb
l	liter	metric unit of volume or 1.057 qt
lb	pound	457 g or 16 oz
µg	microgram	one-millionth of a gram or 0.000001 g
µU	microunit	one-millionth of a unit, e.g., 0.00000001 cc
mg	milligram	one-thousandth of a gram or 0.001 g or 0.000035 oz
ml	milliliter	one-thousandth of a liter or 0.001 liter or 1 cc
oz	ounce	28.35 g or 0.0625 lb
pt	pint	0.473 liter or 0.5 qt (1 pound water)
qt	quart	2 pt or 0.955 liter
U	unit	adopted standard quantity

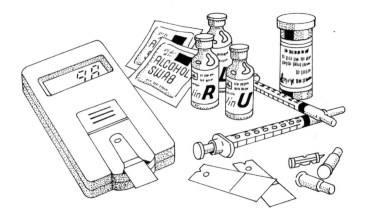

Chapter 2

Life Begins to Change for Me

The day following my diagnosis of diabetes mellitus was a long and fatiguing one. I went to school until noon and then headed to Dr. Martin Draznin's office with mom. Dad arrived a little later after work.

Dr. Draznin talked about how most other youth newly diagnosed with diabetes went to the hospital for a week or two, to learn the physical skills they would need for the rest of their lives. All patients and their families are not the same, he told me. His experience as a pediatric endocrinologist had taught him that he needed to individualize diabetes care education to each family and

their needs. So he was going to start doing everything with me as an outpatient as he had with
other young people. I was clearly not a guinea pig,
and my family had confidence in his judgment.

Both Dr. Draznin and my parents thought I
would be afraid; they found it odd that I was
much happier that I did not have to spend a week
or two in the hospital—that would have been
another week or two out of an already shaky high
school start. I was excited and felt unique to have
gotten diabetes, but of course I did not know then
what was fully involved.

During that long post-diagnosis day, September 28, 1993, I learned everything that I needed

in order to survive until my next visit. I was bombarded with information, techniques, and the consequences of having diabetes.

I learned first what causes diabetes mellitus. My pancreas was not producing enough insulin so that the food I ate was not being processed normally.

Instead of the digested food being stored as fuel for later use by my body, the simple sugars stayed in my bloodstream. And because my body was getting energy by burning stored fats, rather than food carbohydrates, ketones were building up there, too. Finally, both the sugar and ketones in my blood spilled into my urine during their passage through my kidneys. That accounted for my high blood sugar counts and the sugar and ketones that Dr. Feinberg had found in my urine.

Karyl Hare, the diabetes educator at the office, did most of the work in helping me. What a ton of information! First she explained the different kinds of insulin medications I would need to buy and their very specific effects on my body. Then she showed me how to test my blood sugar with a glucometer, to draw up insulin into a syringe, to give myself insulin injections, and to read urine paper test strips. She taught me about glucometer readings of blood sugar levels and what the different levels mean. I was grateful that she was so patient with me and my parents.

My body, like yours, can't sense any difference in the insulin produced by a pancreas from insulin bottled by pharmaceutical companies and bought at the drug store. This is all so basic to me now, but at the time my head was spinning and I felt completely overwhelmed.

All that information took a long time to communicate and even start to sink into my head. My blood sugar level was 585 mg/dl before I received my first insulin shot. I particularly remember being extremely drowsy and almost falling asleep immediately before the injection.

We were in the office seven hours. During this time I also spoke to the dietitian, Susan Larner, but she spoke mostly with my mom. Dr. Draznin spoke mostly with my dad. The doctor and dietician spoke with me as well, but I was concentrating on how to do the basic things that Karyl had taught me. I thought they were the most important at that stage.

When I left the office, crowded in front of my mind was all I had been taught to do, but in the back of my mind was the haunting fear of

what my first insulin reaction was going to feel like. They had mentioned "unconscious" and "glucagon injection," both of which really caught my attention. That evening my family went to dinner at Elias' Brothers Big Boy restaurant, and I came home feeling much stronger. I hit the sack all ready for school the next day (or so I thought).

NOTES

Have you ever wondered how the medical professionals on TV shows can respond so quickly to urgent situations? In real life it is because of two factors—*principles* (of anatomy, physiology, and chemistry) and *practice* (through many opportunities to apply those principles). Although body fluid testing may seem complicated at first, take it step by step. Soon you will be a "pro" too!

BODY FLUID TESTING

Blood Testing

1. Have clean hands. Use an alcohol swab.

2. Get blood to the fingers by rubbing hands together, running them under warm water, or "milking" the blood in the finger. Squeeze the finger between the hand and the tip.

3. Use an Ultra-Fine™ lancet, one with a very sharp but thin cutting point.
   Lancets, in blade or needle forms, are meant for pricking the skin. They are individually packaged inside protective plastic caps in quantities of 100-200 per box by many manufacturers and distributors. Most fit into more than one of several brands of ergonomic lancing devices, like, Penlet®, Glucolet®, Hemaletô, Dialetô, Softclix®. They allow handling the pricking tool with ease and safety. Sold separately, these devices range in price from $15-$35, while the average retail cost for lancets is less than nine cents each.

4. Make finger poke on the outside of the finger tip. Avoid the pad of your finger with its many nerve endings.

5. Quickly put blood drop on strip. Exposure to air may give false high counts.

6. Firmly press site with clean tissue while your glucometer is calculating the test result.

Although shelf prices range from $20-$120 for various glucometer styles with digital readouts and a wide range of computational functions, rebates are widespread. Rebates and trade-ins on new instruments come as coupon offers from local pharmacies, hospital supply companies, and e-commerce firms. Some kits include lancing devices. All manufacturers include toll-free phone numbers to connect buyers with customer service representatives to help in emergency medical situations or to explain the proper use of this tool. Your doctor and nurse can help you choose the right meter—remember, diabetes care is personal and individualized—and train you to use it properly.

7. Dispose of the lancet in a Sharps container or in a compartment of your testing kit until a Sharps container is available. Do this at least to keep from cutting yourself and to protect others from any blood-borne disease you may have. Sharps containers are labeled "biohazard" because a disease agent that threatens to harm humans may have contaminated the used lancets or needles you put into them.

Urine Testing

1. Dip test strip in urine; or for less hassle, place the strip in the urine stream.

2. Read substance levels at the exact times recommended on the container.

Screening the urine for critical substances can be done with reagent strips ("dipsticks") or with reagent tablets. *Reagents* are chemical substances that cause a very specific chemical reaction to occur in the presence of certain other substances. They serve to detect, measure, examine, or produce other substances. Reagents that change color are *chromagens*, from Greek words meaning "color producers," and when their color changes indicate how much of a substance is present, they are *colormetric* or "color measurers."

Although urine testing kits for glucose and/or ketones are still commonly available in drug stores, most health care professionals recommend them **only** for ketones to avoid accidents. Sometimes patients have mistakenly used a urine glucose strip when thinking they were testing for ketones. Their calls for instruction for taking extra insulin to bring the reading down resulted in too much insulin producing severe hypoglycemia.

An unconventional use for urine glucose strips is for testing sauces and soft drinks to verify that they really don't have sugar in them. Eating out could be a problem: if drinks get mixed up, results can be drastic. Just test yours to be sure. If the strip turns dark green, the food contains sugar. Always carrying a bottle of strips with you is inexpensive insurance.

Other dangers are possible with urine glucose tablets. They can cause serious burns if toddlers ingest them. Keep your family life simple—use urine tests for ketones only, and blood tests for sugar levels.

SUBSTANCE TESTS IN BLOOD AND URINE

You know the power of color if you have tinkered with a chemistry set at home, used food coloring to dye Easter eggs, or dyed your hair. Chemistry makes use of that knowledge and is the foundation for substance tests.

Blood Sugar Levels

The digital readouts on the glucometer will show how much glucose is in your blood. Read the number and mentally add the metric unit label mg/dl. Here is what these amounts mean:

Over 240 mg/dl   Needs attention NOW

160 to 240 mg/dl   Needs attention
Change routine tomorrow

120 to 160 mg/dl   Bears watching
Not unusual after meals

80 to 120 mg/dl   Ideal—target range

65 to 80 mg/dl   Low but safe

60 to 65 mg/dl   Low
Danger of hypoglycemia

Below 60 mg/dl   Too low
Hypoglycemia

A drop of blood positioned on a blood test strip is all a battery-operated glucometer needs to calculate the weight of glucose in a deciliter of whole blood (less than 3.5 fluid ounces or not even as much liquid as a small juice glass holds). Laboratory levels above 65 mg/dl plasma glucose are safe, and many meters measure whole blood glucose which is lower than plasma glucose by 12%.

Hooking a blood test strip into a glucometer puts your drop in contact with a reagent-soaked pad that must be kept dry before use. Bottles of reagent strips are capped with silica gel to absorb function-destroying moisture; they should be kept out of the refrigerator, but not above a temperature of 86° Fahrenheit. These strips in an opened and capped bottle have a shelf-life of about four months.

Reagent-pad ingredients in blood test strips include the enzymes glucose oxidase and peroxidase. Words ending with -ase are usually enzymes; they always break something down. Glucose oxidase functions the same way whether it is working inside your body or on a reagent pad. It combines with oxygen in the air to break down glucose, producing gluconic acid and some peroxide (the same substance you may have used to bleach your hair or disinfect a scraped knee). Peroxidase reacts with the peroxide and acid produced in the first half-reaction, breaking them down to mostly water and causing the reagent pad to change color.

Urine Sugar Levels

The normal amount of glucose in urine is less than or equal to 0.3 g over 24 hours, effectively a negative reading in both adults and children. In insulin-dependent diabetics, a negative urine test result could correspond to a wide range of blood glucose levels. Glucose in urine, or *glucosuria*, usually occurs when the blood glucose level is greater than 180-200 mg/dl. Both urination and thirst increase at these levels.

People spill sugar into their urine at different blood sugar levels, so the meaning of a urine sugar test is often confusing. Urine test results may be misleading, while home blood glucose monitoring is more accurate.

Urine Ketone Levels

Urine ketones appear in the urine when body tissue, particularly fat, is being broken down for energy because not enough food has been eaten or not enough insulin is present

to help the body burn sugar.
- A trace reading means body tissues are beginning to be burned for energy. Normally sugar would be the energy source.
- The higher the readings, the longer and more severe the abnormal *metabolism* has been occurring. In other words, your body has been burning its own tissues for a long time when it should have been burning sugar. This can be very damaging to you.

Ketone build-up in the body can cause a medical emergency, ketoacidosis, that can produce unconsciousness and may require hospitalization. Urine ketones must be detected early before this crisis occurs—something easily accomplished by self-testing methods at home or away. If results show moderate or large amounts of ketones present, call your doctor or diabetic educator immediately!

Ketone checks are needed under any one of these conditions, according to Dr. H. Peter Chase:

1. New diagnosis of diabetes — Check twice daily or more often if urine ketones are positive. If all ketone checks during the first two weeks are negative, discontinue them.

2. One insulin injection per day — Check morning urine ketones to find out if your insulin is lasting a full 24 hours.

3. Morning blood sugars vary between very high and very low — Check morning urine ketones to find out if your blood sugar is "rebounding" or "bouncing" after a low during the night. Your body responds to these lows by releasing two hormones (adrenaline and glucagon) to raise the blood sugar level. These hormones can put ketones in the urine.

4. High blood sugars — Check urine ketones if your blood sugar is more than 240 mg/dl.

5. Anytime a diabetic feels sick — Check urine

ketones especially if vomiting occurs. When sickness develops, ketones can be present even if the blood sugar is **not** high.

Urine Ketone Test Strips

Two strips most frequently used are Ketostix® and Chemstrip®K. They differ primarily in how long the fresh urine is exposed to reagent before you read the color change results, according to the color blocks printed on the package insert. Mental counting is not good enough. Accurate timing to the second is necessary. Ketostix® requires exactly 15 seconds; Chemstrip®K, 60 seconds.

Individual foil-wrapped test strips are better, although more expensive, than bottles of test strips because they are reliable for a longer time. The foil wrapping prevents their exposure to moisture in the air. Their expiration date may be two years from the time they were packaged, instead of six months.

Urine Ketone Tablets

Accurate timing is also crucial to reading Acetest® tablet results; 30 seconds is necessary. Tablet color changes are gradations of purple.

INSULIN INJECTIONS

How much insulin to inject is based on body weight and the results of blood sugar tests. The right dose starts with measuring the insulin in units, where 100 units has the volume of 1 cc. Dosage usually starts at one-fourth unit per pound (0.25 U/lb) or one-half unit per kilogram (0.5 U/kg). It may go up to 1 U/kg or 1 unit every 2 lb.

In rapidly growing adolescents however, insulin doses about 1U/kg are not unusual. The higher level of growth hormone circulating through a teen's body causes an increased need for insulin. Growth hormone is a counter regulatory hormone that protects against low blood sugar when fasting, for example, during nighttime sleep.

Regardless of the amount needed, use these steps to inject your insulin:
1. Clean the tops of insulin bottles with alcohol swab.

2. Acquire a sterilized syringe.

3. Draw up desired dose by injecting the same amount of units of air into each bottle for the units of insulin to be drawn out of that bottle. Remember to not allow air bubbles into the syringe by keeping the needle tip submerged in the insulin.

Draw up the short-acting insulins first, such as Humalog® or Regular. Then be sure that the long-acting insulins are mixed adequately by rolling the bottle gently. Draw up the longer-acting insulins second, whether NPH, Lente®, or Ultralente®.

4. Clean the site of injection with alcohol swab and then let it air dry. Do not blow on the site to speed up the drying time. That can add germs to the site.

5. Pinch up the *subcutaneous tissue* found just underneath the skin of the chosen site. Be sure to *rotate the injection sites*, that is, choose a different site than either your previous injection or your next one in a regular pattern you can remember.

By rotating the site, the previous site heals from a past shot and can be reused over and over throughout life. Suggestions for managing site rotation are to focus on one large area, for example, the thigh, and within that large area use as many separate sites as possible while keeping the injections no closer to each other than one and a half inches.

6. While pinching the subcutaneous tissue with a non-dominant hand, hold the syringe like a pen in the dominant hand. Thrust the needle completely, all the way up to its hilt, into the site. To avoid more pain than necessary, do this step quickly. If the needle is first touched to the skin and then injected slowly, a stinging pain can result.

Keep in mind that you will only feel the needle go

through your skin. Once past the skin, you won't feel it. Pinching your flesh will make it hard to feel the needle at all. If you do hit a nerve occasionally, you will feel it right away so you can choose another site immediately.

7. Once the needle is completely in, relax the squeezed tissue and get ready to inject the insulin.

8. Injecting the insulin should be done slowly. Put in approximately five units; wait a few seconds. Then put in five more and wait a few more seconds, and so on. This helps preserve the site and, even though the needle is in the skin longer, it is actually less painful.

9. When all the insulin has been injected, pull the needle straight out, cap it, and dispose of it properly, most likely into a Sharps container.

As newspaper readers of Ann Landers' columns should know, insulin injections can occur unobtrusively in public places. Often nobody sitting at the same restaurant table even notices. There is no need to pull up one's shirt and expose skin. Diabetics can inject right through clothing. However, doing this can lead to strange tattoos as pieces of cloth get trapped under the skin. Another possible consequence is that newer, very thin needles may bend or break off in the skin if they are handled roughly.

Injection Review
- Sterilize the bottle cap.
- Obtain the syringe.
- Draw up the insulin.
- Choose a site and clean it.
- Pinch up skin.
- Insert needle quickly.
- Relax the tissue
- Inject insulin slowly.
- Remove and cap the needle.
- Dispose of the needle properly.

Chapter 3

That First Hypoglycemic Episode

The next day I awoke at 6:00 a.m. after a good night's sleep (no getting up to go to the bathroom—hooray!) and, as instructed, called my doctor right away for my insulin dosage. I remember being completely baffled as to how he chose the right amount. I had no understanding about the number of units he told me to take. I took the given amount, waited a half hour, and ate my breakfast.

On the previous morning, breakfast had not been a problem. I just ate a bowl of Apple Jacks® and that was all the more I thought of it. This morning was slightly more complicated. Now I had to concentrate on how many starches were in my cereal, how much milk to put on it, should I have a fruit, did I need protein? All these questions, as anyone with diabetes knows, we ask ourselves before every meal. It was very confusing that morning, and I felt like I was lost.

Once the puzzling and difficult task of breakfast was done, I was off to school. I was rather excited because, however confusing it was, I was intrigued by the novelty of it all. And, in my excitement about regained strength, I had already forgotten how pooped out and headachy I had felt the last several weeks.

I also specifically remember not telling any of my friends. It was not out of fear or embarrassment. I was just not comfortable with revealing it yet. I hardly understood the disease.

> **"I checked my blood sugar... and it was 50! I had no idea what to do; my brain had left me."**

There would have been no way I could have answered anyone's questions correctly. I did, however, tell my teachers in case I would ever have an insulin reaction.

Everything went smoothly until my fourth hour class. About halfway through it, I was given permission to go to the bathroom. On the way back I felt a little different, light-headed and getting flushed. I went back to class and told my

teacher I was going to the administration office. Once I got there, I checked my blood sugar and it was 50! I had no idea what to do; my brain had left me. I felt really spaced out.

Somehow it occurred to me to call my diabetes educator. Karyl told me to eat three glucose tablets, which I did while she stayed on the phone, and then I just ate my bag lunch in the administration office with all the secretaries and staff. Lo and behold, the weird feeling went away.

Not knowing then why my blood sugar had been at 50 mg/dl, I felt scared that I had lost control of my own body. However, I soon learned that I only needed to make some small adjust-

ments in order to balance things out. That's right—small, step-by-step adjustments. Dad would tell me, "You don't want to steer so hard to get out of the ditch on the right-hand side of the road that you end up in the left-hand ditch."

NOTES

HYPOGLYCEMIA

What Is It?

Hypoglycemia means the blood sugar level is too low to carry on normal metabolism. If severe lows occur often enough, brain cells die off. Hypoglycemia is a serous problem.

Sometimes it is called an *insulin reaction* or *insulin shock* because your body is reacting to the impact that an overdose of insulin produces. This usually occurs at some level below 65 mg/dl. Low blood sugar readings can take place at any time, so whenever you are away from home, be prepared to combat a hypoglycemic reaction by planning ahead.

"Be very aware of earlier signs... treat yourself before a crisis happens."

The first time hypoglycemia occurs you could easily pass out because you don't have past experience with it.

Some people report frequent symptoms of low blood sugar for different reasons. If blood sugar levels run higher than normal for a long period, any fall in blood sugar will feel like a "low," even though it's not low. In these cases the body became used to the higher level. Low blood sugar symptoms occur either because blood sugar falls rapidly, for example,

27

from 300 mg/dl to 150 mg/dl, or because blood sugar is truly low, for example, less than 60 mg/dl. A blood sugar check will help you decide which of these causes is responsible.

Possible Symptoms

> "Always wear your Medical Alert identifier with instructions for unconsciousness."

- Light-headed, faint feeling, dizziness
- Shakiness
- Sweatiness or feeling flushed ("head sweats")
- Weakness
- Hunger
- Mental confusion
- Convulsions
- Unconsciousness

Symptoms can occur very suddenly, with absolutely no warning signs. They happen so fast. One teen said his hands tingled before he became disoriented and could not stand up.

What Can I Do About It?

Think Ahead

First of all, always wear your Medical Alert tag or bracelet to indicate that you have insulin-

FRONT
NAME HERE
EMERGENCY PHONE

DIABETES
HOME ADDRESS
HOME PHONE
MEDICATIONS, ALLERGIES
DOCTOR NAME
DOCTOR PHONE

BACK

dependent diabetes mellitus, give instructions for unconsciousness, and identify both yourself and your health care provider.

Thinking ahead also means preparing your companions for possible problems. Let them know where they can find help, like your Medical Alert tag and what it means.

Whether you eat or not, the injected insulin you've taken will be working to lower your blood sugar. Avoiding hypoglycemia means eating regularly, so take along glucose tabs, juice, or whatever works best for you. Snacks help balance insulin activity.

Treat Myself

Preparing yourself and friends around you for your possible bouts with hypoglycemia allows you to manage outcomes with confidence. Panic doesn't cut it. A person with diabetes who lets his blood sugar get low must raise it:

- *Eat any fast-acting sugar,* for example
  Glucose tabs*
  Regular soda pop, fruit juice, or fruit
  Candy, cookies, Pop Tarts®, *OR*
- *Eat any other food* in an emergency.**
- *Rest* to minimize sugar burning.

* Glucose tabs and fruit juice work much faster than candy or cookies. Glucose tabs, containing dextrose, various fruit flavorings, and tablet-binding agents, come packaged as chewable tablets. A typical dose is two or three tablets to stop reaction episodes that may be caused by longer-acting insulins. You can expect tablets sold by brand name *vs.* those available under chain store names to cost more than per tablet (for example, 6¢ *vs.* 4¢), but they also weigh more (5 g *vs.* 4 g each). Printed on some brand name package labels is a toll-free emergency phone number.

** Of course, you cannot do this if your symptoms have progressed to unconsciousness. Be very aware of the earlier signs, and treat yourself before a crisis happens. If a blood sugar test shows between 60-100 mg/dl or a rapid fall causes your symptoms, food *not* high in sugar may work.

Depend upon Someone Else

Friends become increasingly important to teenagers. Along with family and teachers, they must know what to do when someone succumbs to hypoglycemia. These are responsible actions:

A. *Apply frosting or any sugar paste,* like cake decorating gel in tubes, with your fingers to the inside of the stricken person's cheek lining between the gums and inner cheek. Rub the area so sugars from the paste can be absorbed by the unconscious patient. This is possible because, even without swallowing, the unconscious person's saliva digests the sugar and allows it to be absorbed into the bloodstream by the blood vessels lining the cheek.

Emergency first-aid training has long cautioned against putting anything in the mouth of a semi- or unconscious person. A reasonable concern is that the unconscious may breathe the substance in and choke instead of ideally swallowing it. Health care professionals continue to be quite nervous about this action, and are not convinced that gels work that well.

A temporary excess of sugar won't make a person with diabetes sick. It will just be passed into the urine. Long-term health complications, however, do occur because of routine poor control of blood sugar.

B. *Get a syringe of glucagon* out of the unconscious patient's carrying case, and read the instructions. Teen diabetics should always carry this emergency treatment if they are prone to hypoglycemic reactions that stretch to actual unconsciousness and should instruct their family, teachers or companions in its use.

Glucagon is a stress hormone, also made naturally in the pancreas, to regulate the conversion of glycogen, the stored form of glucose, back to glucose. As glycogen is made, it removes glucose from the blood, thereby lowering blood sugar levels. Glucagon does just the opposite. When the body needs to put more sugar into the blood, glucagon causes the liver to release glucose into the bloodstream, stimulating an increase in blood sugar levels. Upon injection, glucagon quickly raises blood sugar levels. This drugstore purchase must be kept below 90º F. It can be stored at room temperature or in the refrigerator. On trips, put it in a cooler, along with bottles of insulin and blood sugar test strips.

C. Seek emergency medical help. Always do A and B (above) first. Check blood sugar levels second, and then get medical help. Call the emergency number on the stricken person's Medical Alert tag or bracelet; if none is being worn, call 911 in areas where it is available.

METABOLISM AND STRESS

Metabolism

Metabolism is the balanced way our bodies' cells chemically change food to keep us alive. When digested food is burned (meaning, combined with oxygen) to release its stored energy that powers body activities, this metabolic food breakdown is called *catabolism*. When the products of digestion are used to build or mend cells, this metabolic assembly is called *anabolism*. Insulin is required for both kinds of metabolism.

A body's *basal metabolism rate* (BMR) is the minimum amount of energy required to maintain vital functions in a fasting individual who is awake and resting comfortably in a warm environment. It consumes 75% of your body's total energy output. This energy takes the form of heat, and the production of heat mirrors the rate of oxygen used.

Stress

Stress is a part of normal daily living. It speeds up metabolism when problems we face change the way we feel to worry, excitement, or being upset or scared. Stress causes production of adrenaline and glucagon that raise blood sugar levels and break down fat. Anyone with diabetes needs to be aware that the "fight or flight" hormone *adrenaline* breaks down muscle glycogen, the starch that is stored

31

Diabetes at 14

sugar. Adrenaline keeps blood sugar up during exercise and may cause increased urine sugar.

Stress is part of being a teenager when bodily changes include emerging sexuality. Emotional swings change blood adrenaline levels, and eating habits may reflect those emotions. Managing a chronic illness during these years just adds more than the usual amount of stress. Family medical insurance may cover part of the costs for individual or group counseling to help deal with it. This kind of counseling is a very useful part of total diabetes management.

Balance

Balance means being a whole person—physically, emotionally, socially, spiritually—at whatever age. Balance is more than managing insulin, meal planning, and exercise. Wellness and empowerment are part of the picture.

Teens and young children with diabetes, like their parents and grandparents, invite infinite possibilities for meaningful lives when they accept themselves as persons, maintain a positive self concept, adapt to changes, ask questions or seek help, and advocate for themselves.

Young people with diabetes do not ever have to think that diabetes has ruined their lives and caused them to be unhealthy. They need to know that they are normal, healthy, independent, smart individuals. With parents who support their child's development of confidence and positive thinking, young diabetics can learn that they are people first and much more than just a disease. Diabetes does not have to stop them from doing anything.

32

Chapter 4

Learning to Plan Ahead

Going off to school in the morning became much more difficult after I developed diabetes. I had to make sure I had the right supplies before leaving home so I would be prepared for any change in course.

Every morning after testing my blood and taking my morning insulin, I would put all my daily supplies in a pile and run through my mental check list before putting them in my book bag's special compartments. The list included glucometer, test strips, lancets, Penlet®, logbook, and pen. Later on I began taking three shots per day, so I added alcohol swabs and a syringe al-

ready drawn up with insulin to the list. All of
these items were much more easily transported

once I got a carrying case designed specifically for
diabetic supplies. It simplified my awareness of
what supplies I had with me and which ones I did
not.

In addition, the checklist included glucose
tablets, just in case I developed a hypoglycemic
reaction, and an easily transportable snack. Now I
know that other young people with diabetes never

leave home without food or drink. Early on I
made it a habit of setting the timer on my wrist-
watch for snack time so I would not forget it. Most
importantly, I could concentrate on life and not
worry about forgetting the snack.

Mental Checklist

- Glucometer
- Test strips
- Lancets
- Penlet®
- Logbook
- Pen
- Alcohol swabs
- Syringe
- Insulin
- Glucose tablets
- Cake decorating icing
- Transportable snack

This was adequate planning all fall and
winter of my freshman year until spring. I decided
then that my shoulder was healed from the surgery and I wanted to go out for the tennis team

which held practices every day after school. Since I never went home between dismissal and practices or matches, I needed to prepare in the morning. I fixed a hearty snack and some emergency food (in case of a hypoglycemic reaction) that would not require refrigeration nor much protection. It had to be such that it could be digested quickly so I would not get a gut ache during practice.

All of this was tough to integrate into my schedule, but whenever I neglected it, I could not manage my diabetes smoothly or enjoy my activities. I soon learned: I must take care of myself.

NOTES

DIABETIC SUPPLY SOURCES

Carrying cases like the one I use for convenient self-injection, monitoring my sugar levels, possible emergency treatments, and all the instruments and medications to do these things, can sometimes be purchased from local pharmacies for $5-$30. When your corner drugstore does not stock some item you want, check the telephone book's Yellow Pages for new possibilities under these headings:
Diabetic Products
Medical Equipment & Supplies
Pharmacies

Search Engine	Virtual Store	Geographic Location
Alta Vista	MediQuik Services	Texas
	Oxystat Home Health	Florida
	Richmond Apothecaries	Virginia
Excite	Diabetes Card Services	Michigan
	Diabetes Home Care	Florida
	Planet RX	California
Hot Bot	Diabetes Club	Washington
	Fifty 50 Pharmacy	Texas
	Supermed, Inc.	Florida
Yahoo	Express-Med	Ohio
	Medicool	California
	National Diabetic Pharmacies	Virginia

You can also turn to virtual stores on the Internet, should you have a credit card. Virtual sources found today might be gone tomorrow, but different search engines that index e-commerce sites may help. For example, *see* table above.

SNACKS

Remember "a little something" from *Winnie-the-Pooh*? Snacks help balance insulin activity. Small amounts of readily available food are important if meals cannot be served on time or if you are sick and your body needs more energy to fight infection. These extra calories will prevent your body from breaking down fat and producing ketonuria.

How different are the kinds of snacks you eat now with Type I diabetes from those you probably ate as a non-diabetic? This is a very tricky question.

Candy bars and ice cream are still okay to eat, but only when done at the right time and in the right amount. Do not eat them unless they are essential; they are not "treats." I eat them only when I am already involved in an activity and my blood sugar is low because I did not eat enough other food before the exercise or I'm working harder than I had anticipated. As a means of regulating my blood sugar in these situations, I pick something that is fast, like juice, a few crackers, or an occasional candy bar, to last me until my activity ends.

The type of snack depends on the expected length of planned exercise activity. Fruits are good daytime snacks because the sugar from them will only last one or two hours. Longer-term activities will require snacks that also include complex carbohydrates (starches), like crackers or bread. Bedtime snacks to last through the night must absorb slowly, so a solid protein works best then.

Easily Transportable Snacks
- Fruit cookies (for example, fig bars)
- Breakfast bars
- Juices
- Sports drinks

These pre-athletic snacks are great for light, short periods of activity. They are good because their nutrients are absorbed quickly into the bloodstream and do not hang around once the short activity is done. None of them requires refrigeration either.

Hearty Snacks

Nutrients in hearty snacks absorb more slowly. Snacks that keep the blood sugar up the longest include a protein, a fat, and a carbohydrate. Because they are in your system for a much longer time, you can count on needing fewer snack breaks to maintain enough energy for long-term activities.

- Sandwiches with a light protein
- Graham crackers/animal crackers and milk
- Saltines and cottage cheese

They might be a cheese or meat sandwich with a glass of juice. "Might be" means that only your own experiences can confirm what's right for you. Keeping a record of your blood sugar numbers from a glucometer before and after exercise, snacks, and meals, will help you learn this lesson.

CARBOHYDRATE LOADING

Carbohydrates are foods that provide energy by supplying immediate calories. They are the sugars, starches, cellulose, and related compounds that primarily contain the chemical elements carbon, hydrogen, and oxygen. *Carbohydrate loading* is eating extra quantities of high-starch foods like rice, breads, potatoes, and pasta to increase carbohydrate reserves in muscle tissue. Some marathoners and other endurance athletes follow this dietary practice before competitions.

Early in my diabetic life, long-term athletic activities proved the most difficult situations to manage. All I really knew in the beginning was that my body used sugar when I exercised, so eating something sweet beforehand should keep me "safe." However, if the sport lasted longer than 15 or 20 minutes, I would need something sweet again. My blood sugar was constantly going up and down, and my body would have to recover from "lows" multiple times. This

39

way of managing blood sugar does work, but is far from ideal.

Stopping whatever I was doing, eating, and waiting for the food to "kick-in"—what a bother! By the time I regained enough energy to continue or go back into the game—as in basketball—I would find myself not as responsive, quick, or precise as I had been previously. I just wanted to compete and have fun, but instead I had to concentrate on whether or not I needed to eat. A method that took care of my blood sugar before I got into a game or activity and allowed me to focus on my performance, not diabetes, would solve this problem

Carbohydrate loading was, and is, the best solution for me. I was at first concerned about eating large amounts of food prior to a game because I thought it would make me cramp up or sluggish. Experiments with different combinations of starch and protein, however, taught me differently. Eating a peanut butter and jelly sandwich and taking no extra insulin before practice or a game combined to balance my blood sugar with my basal insulin for the activity itself.

This proved a better way for me manage than when I used to add sugar as needed. With carbohydrate loading, sugar was being released into my bloodstream at a slow constant rate, provoking less stress and body damage.

It's a chore to find out what food works best. Everyone will be different, but some sort of carbohydrate and possibly a light protein—the peanut butter in my case—is usually the best way to go. This method of management has made my sporting events, as well as any activity, less worrisome. Consequently, much more enjoyment re-entered my life.

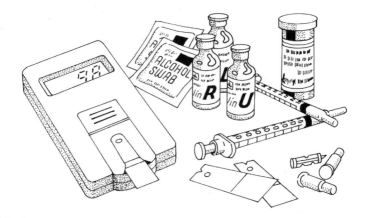

Chapter 5

School Adjustments

During the first month or so that I had diabetes, every time I wished to check my blood sugar or eat a snack, I had to leave the classroom. I

did not have a problem with this early on because, honestly, it gave me an excuse to cut class. However, after a month of that, I started to realize that missing about five minutes of class, while it did not seem very long, began to add up quickly. When keeping up in class got harder, I explained to my teachers that I would be doing diabetic duties in class from then on.

Of course, my school, like many schools, had a policy that all medicines had to be taken in the supervised administration area. The administration was reluctant to make an exception. You know how it is—they want you to grow up, but still treat you like a child. I had to argue with the vice principal that complying with that rule would mean a lot of missed class time for something that was not distracting to anyone else. Certainly I would not allow that to happen. With my parents' backing my decision, he finally consented.

From then on I merely told my teachers at the beginning of each semester, "I have diabetes. Occasionally I'll have to test my blood, give myself a shot, or eat a snack in class." No teacher objected as long as there was no disturbance and I cleaned up after myself—which I did by putting the lancet, blood sample, and syringe into the waste pocket of my carrying case. Other things I did to avoid

making a scene were turning off the "beep" mode on my glucometer and taking my insulin in a way that did not attract attention, usually by lifting my shirt in a quiet manner and injecting around my abdomen. I just realized that this was what I had to do, even though it might bother other people. All of us need to take responsibility for our own actions and feelings.

Doing my blood tests and injections in class were important battles to win for three reasons: they allowed me to stay competitive and on track in school; I could regulate such a personalized disease on the schedule set by my body; and, they brought me one step closer towards a life with freedom.

NOTES

SCHOOL POLICIES

Health Care Team

Who belongs on a health care team? First, list the student and then his or her family. Add everyone at school who comes in contact with the student: bus drivers, teachers, coaches, the school nurse if the district has one, plus a diabetes educator and/or dietitian, doctors, and office nurses. Don't forget the janitorial staff who frequently have casual informal relationships with students. Each one plays a role, and good communication among them helps students the most.

> **Guidelines developed jointly by health care professionals focus on the student with diabetes.**

Sometimes the student's family gives the bus driver and sports coaches a can of juice to keep in their first-aid boxes. Sending extra juice boxes to stock the student's locker for quick access by prepared teachers also may be an appropriate precaution to prevent hypoglycemic incidents during the school day.

The American Diabetes Association and Johns Hopkins Hospital developed guidelines in 1991 for school policies. They specified providing handwashing facilities, a private space, and containers for Sharps disposal as part of in-school management of blood glucose monitoring, insulin injections, meal planning, hypoglycemia, and ketoacidosis.

When school begins, parents should meet with teachers and the school nurse to discuss the following:
- The student's Individualized Health Plan
- A plan to keep staff and family informed
- Symptoms of an insulin reaction
- Treatment for insulin reactions—extra snacks, use of glucose or glycogen
- Nutrition needs—lunch, extra snacks, foods at class parties
- Appropriate school schedule
- Bathroom privileges
- Blood glucose monitoring
- Coordinating food with exercise
- Needs on school bus, field trips, other activities

Prior to the rise of intensive insulin therapy, advocated by health care professionals in the 1990s, children with diabetes took injections once or twice a day, usually not in school. Low blood sugar concerned school staff most, and they tended to overprotect the child to prevent it. Overprotection was both unnecessary and undesirable. It tended to postpone development of the child's independence and self-esteem, and encouraged the development of prolonged hyperglycemia (high blood sugar levels) and serious complications later in life.

We now know that intensive insulin therapy reduces the risk of diabetic complications. It requires frequent self-monitoring of blood glucose levels, either continuous infusion with a pump or multiple injections sometimes during the day, and perhaps snacks between meals. The student can test and treat himself in less than two minutes, with little distraction to the classroom environment. School personnel need to learn modern methods of diabetic management rather than overprotect or embarrass the student with discriminatory policies, statements, and/or behaviors.

47

Some school districts used to or may still prohibit students from doing blood sugar testing on school property. They had teachers send a child who felt hypoglycemic to the school nurse. Then the nurse called a parent to come from home or work with a family-owned glucometer to test the child's blood sugar. The child, unaccompanied by a classmate, might miss 30 minutes to an hour of instruction. This policy denies the student an equal education opportunity, a safe educational environment, and full access to the educational process. Other districts prohibit students from taking insulin injections while on school property, in spite of physician's recommendations. They risk litigation.

Legislative Support

The risk-prone policy examples given above violate federal civil rights laws: the Rehabilitation Act, Section 504 (RA, 1973), with guidelines for negotiated written plans; the Americans with Disabilities Act, Titles II and III (ADA, 1990), which includes private schools; and, the Individuals with Disabilities Education Act (IDEA, 1992), that ensures the right to request appropriate accommodations.

IDEA specifically covers children with diabetes under "chronic health conditions." Both RA, Sec. 504, and IDEA apply to any school receiving federal financial aid. Parents have the right to request accommodations in negotiated written plans with school administrators and to be present whenever the written plan is reviewed or changed before the change is implemented. Accommodations might include eating whenever and wherever necessary, going to the drinking fountain or bathroom, participating fully in all extra-curricular activities, and assisting with blood glucose monitoring or insulin injections where appropriate.

Both the American Diabetes Association and the Juvenile Diabetes Foundation offer parent-teacher presentations on request to educate school personnel about diabetes. They suggest that regular or substitute teachers, the school nurse, and the school office all need a list of emergency contacts. These events help satisfy the legal requirements for accommodation; they cost no money, but do require a few hours of faculty time.

School districts must provide training to every teacher and other school personnel who come in contact with diabetic students, approximately one of every 600 in school. Failure to provide such training, especially upon parental request, may result in termination of federal assistance and legal action for damage and fees against the school district, under RA and ADA.

School personnel face legal liability when implementing or supervising routines advocated for students with diabetes. Allowing blood sugar testing in school appears to conflict with the need to protect school employees and other students from blood exposure. Teachers cannot take actions that are unnecessary or exceed skills covered by their training. Teachers cannot make medical or treatment judgments for their students. They must all act in a reasonable manner, in accordance with school district-provided training. To ease current concerns, Florida has passed a model law (1992) granting immunity from civil damages to school district personnel who help students in administrating their medications. Other states are seriously considering adopting some version of this Florida law.

INJECTION SITES

Injection sites vary because individuals come in different sizes. Any such site, however, must be easily accessible, as these are:
- Outer area of upper arm
- Just above and below the waist, *except* a two-inch circle around the navel
- Upper area of buttock, just behind the hip bone
- Front of thigh, midway to the outer side
- Four inches below the top of the thigh to four inches above the knee

Which site is best? It depends on your activities; exercise is a factor. If you are a right-handed tennis player, for example, inject into your stomach or buttocks area rather than your upper right arm because insulin absorbs faster when the shot is given in an area subjected to exercise. Remember, low blood sugar may result during exercise.

Chapter 6

Freedom Lost

As all those with diabetes know, good blood sugar regulation does not always come easily. Many things affect the blood sugar level. However, you can learn some tricks to aid enormously in achieving tight blood sugar control. In the beginning of my management, these tricks were much more difficult to incorporate because of the insulin types prescribed by my doctor.

I was on NPH and Regular insulins, just as my doctor had ordered. Patients on this regimen know that they must follow a very strict eating schedule. When I was taking this combination, I did not like several things:

1. NPH has a late peak, which made eating at a specified time in the evening a necessity.

2. I had to wake up by 8 a.m. every morning in order to eat breakfast.

3. I was stuck with a schedule of snacks.

If I wanted to sleep in while taking this insulin, I needed to wake up by 8:00 a.m., take my

 insulin, eat at 8:30 a.m., and then go back to sleep. I did not like this arrangement because once I am awake, it is very difficult for me to go back to sleep. After a late Friday night, I just wanted to sleep in.

Many inconveniences resulted from being on NPH and Regular. A couple of times after school, my friends invited me to go along with them to a JV football or soccer game. However, I

needed a snack, so I needed to go home first.

Sometimes it turned out that I didn't meet back up

with them at the
game, or I had to
leave the game early
to go home for insu-
lin and dinner.

So you can
see, the problem with
this regimen was that
I was on a diet ac-
cording to my insu-
lin. On NPH and Regular you are constantly
eating to control blood sugar levels. Now you
might think that is not so bad, but wouldn't life be
better if you were on insulin according to your
diet? I think so! I wanted a way to be able to eat
the amount I wanted, when I wanted, and then
take insulin accordingly. This would make my life
more flexible and I could avoid being really thin or
really fat.

NOTES

INSULINS

Insulin is the protein hormone formed in the pancreas and secreted into the blood where it does three things:
- Allows cells to burn sugar for energy
- Lowers sugar production in liver and muscle
- Slows fat breakdown

Ever since Canadian scientists first extracted insulin from dogs in the 1920s, newer insulin preparations have been and will certainly continue to be developed because no one kind allows all diabetics to manage their blood sugar

Insulin Durations within the Body

Type of Action	Available Insulins
Very Short	Humalog®
Short	Regular
Intermediate	NPH Lente®
Long	Ultralente®

levels in the same way. People are too different, and the way diabetes affects individuals is very personal. Currently, researchers are looking for a diabetes cure, a way to painlessly monitor blood sugar, and new forms of insulin that could be delivered without injection.

Two obviously different ways to think of insulin types are by length of action—that is, how long they produce results in the body—and by physical form.

Commercial Insulin Development

Type of Action	Available Insulins	Marketed	Physical Form
short	regular zinc	1920s	solution
interme-diate	protamines: PZI= protamine zinc insulin	1930s	suspension in phosphate* buffer
	NPH= neutral protamine Hagedorn	1940s	complex suspension in phosphate* buffer
short	lentes: semilente*		
interme-diate	lente*= mixture of semilente and ultralente	1950s	suspensions in acetate buffer
long	ultralente*		
short	synthetics: humulins	1980s	solutions
very short	Humalog®	1990s	

* **NEVER MIX** phosphate products with lente insulins because phosphate changes solubility of lente crystals. The change in how much dissolves how fast influences how quickly lentes can take effect and how long they last to work on blood sugar levels.

It is also better not to give regular and ultralente or lente in the same syringe because lentes will cause some binding of the regular. Don't mix them together if you dawdle; just use different syringes. Only IF you inject them within three minutes of drawing them up together, should you even think of using the same syringe without negative consequences.

Throughout the 20th century, insulin medications have been given by injection rather than orally. If given orally, this hormone would be digested like any other protein. Only recently have insulins from different companies been compatible. It was prudent to never mix them. All kinds lose activity above 90º F. Finally, regardless of the type and amount you take, insulin affects diet.

DIET

Teens with diabetes, just like all other growing teenagers, need a *well-balanced diet*. This means eating food and drink from all nutrient groups: carbohydrates, proteins, fats, minerals, vitamins, electrolytes, and fibers. Of these, carbohydrates ("carbos") particularly require adequate amounts of insulin. To a lesser degree, insulin is also necessary for using proteins and fats.

Carbohydrate Foods with Absorbable Sugars

A. Foods with *Quickly* Absorbed* Sugars	B . Foods with *Slowly* Absorbed† Sugars
Sugar	Breads
Pastries	Cereal
Milk	Grains
Fruits	Root and pod vegetables, like potatoes and beans

* Absorption happens in a few minutes.
† Absorption takes 10-30 minutes.

Insulin doses should be adjusted according to how much carbohydrate you eat and how fast it can be absorbed into your bloodstream. Frequent testing of blood sugar will determine just how much you should adjust the dose.

After you consume any of the foods listed in Column A (*see* table, previous page), a variety of carbohydrates will be present in your bloodstream within minutes because these foods contain easily convertible sugars or are free, simple sugar already. Sugar in the foods listed in Column B can take 10-30 minutes to appear in your bloodstream because the starches and cellulose in those foods first need to be broken down into simple sugars by the digestive system.

Your body needs protein and fat, too. Meat, fish, milk, and eggs contain large amounts of protein as well as significant portions of fat, which are in a class of materials called lipids. Cholesterol is a blood lipid, 85% of which is produced by our own liver. If we eat foods with less than 30% of our daily calories coming from fat, our body uses it to make the rest of the cholesterol it needs; eating a higher percentage of fat prematurely ages our blood vessels.

People with poorly controlled diabetes have higher blood cholesterol levels than those who have good diabetes control or those who don't have diabetes. When insulin is present, it slows fat breakdown and limits the release of cholesterol. Higher blood cholesterol often results from eating these kinds of foods:
- High in total fat
- High in animal fat
- High in cholesterol

Legumes, like peas and beans, are good sources of plant protein, along with fiber and other complex starches. Fiber produces a "full" feeling during meals. Even though fiber helps the digestive system work smoothly, it is not absorbed by the body. Most of us don't eat enough grains, beans, fresh fruit or veggies to meet the minimum fiber levels recommended by the USDA. Fiber lengthens the time food is in our stomachs. Then, it shortens the time it takes to pass through our intestines, so that both fat and sugar have less time to be absorbed there. For example, combining a glass of fruit juice with a piece of buttered whole wheat toast slows the passage of sugar into the blood.

When you eat any carbohydrate along with a significant amount of soluble fiber, protein, or fat, the absorption process slows down. Absorption starts up again later and is prolonged possibly up to several hours.

Lots of different diets will allow good nutrition and diabetic control of blood sugar. Clarify your options with the dietitian in your health care team. Using this knowledge, you can create meals that allow constant carbohydrate absorption throughout the length of insulin activity that metabolizes components of the food you eat. Another advantage is that if everyone in your family eats the diet best for Type I, insulin-dependent diabetics, you all will be healthier.

FOOD BIOCHEMISTRY

Carbohydrates

Carbohydrates are any or all of the many kinds of sugars, starches, cellulose, and related compounds. They provide energy in the form of calories for all body functions and activities.

All *sugars* have a simple sugar, having molecules with up to seven carbon atoms, as their basic building block. Sucrose (table sugar) and lactose (milk sugar) react very quickly with water in digestive fluids, such as saliva, to form *the simplest sugar, glucose*, with six carbon atoms. Pastries contain those sugars plus fructose, another simple sugar, that is a natural part of fruits and honey. The third simple sugar, galactose, is in lactose but not in other foods.

Starches in grains and vegetables are *complex carbohydrates*. Most pastries and breads are made from flours that are primarily plant starches. Starches (including the animal starch, glycogen), cellulose, and dextrin are known as polysaccharides (literally, from Greek, "many sugars") because each particular kind consists of at least ten

simpler sugars. As animals eat starchy plant foods, the enzyme amylase in their saliva begins to convert the inner portion of a starch granule (the relatively soluble polysaccharide, amylose) to simpler sugars. Other complex sugars in starch, like galactosides, break down to galactose. Once those foods travel through the stomach and into the small intestine, intestinal bacteria and enzymes from the pancreas work on whatever starch is still intact.

Parts of some starches do not dissolve because the glucose units in their molecular structure are in complex, branched form. These insoluble parts contribute to indigestible fiber that animal bodies excrete. *Cellulose*, composed of glucose units joined together by chemical bonds, completely surrounds every cell in most plants. It is the coarse, indigestible ingredient of whole grain breads which provides fiber in your diet.

Proteins

Unlike carbohydrates, *proteins* include an added element, nitrogen, in their molecular structures. However, both proteins and carbohydrates build substances from carbon, hydrogen, and oxygen. Insulin, being a hormone, is a protein. While proteins are found in most kinds of cells, plant and animal, you usually associate them with animal muscle tissue and rightly so. Most plant cells have a much smaller proportion of protein. Egg whites are primarily water mixed with the protein albumin, but egg yolks are mostly fat.

Fats

Fats include the fatty tissue we can easily spot as sometimes conspicuous parts of our own bodies and some poorly trimmed meats. They are also present in the connective tissue that defines certain muscle groups and in seeds, nuts, and fruits of plants. Chemical groups called esters and fatty acids make up fats in living things.

The main fats in our diet are of two types, unsaturated (vegetable oils) and saturated (animal fats). "Saturated" refers to the fat's molecular structure and whether all of its bonding points between elemental atoms are filled with hydrogen atoms. When the molecule cannot bond with any more atoms, it is saturated. Generally, the more liquid a fat is at room temperature, the more unsaturated it is. Unsaturated fats include both poly- and monounsaturated fats.

Chapter 7

Freedom Found

Early in the winter of 1994, I heard about the possibilities of tighter control from Dr. Draznin and my dad. Tighter control means keeping blood sugar levels closer to the "best" target range (80-120 mg/dl). They referred to a large long-term study of insulin-dependent diabetic patients that had just been published in the *New England Journal of Medicine*.

The article described substantially reduced complications for those who took three to four insulin injections *vs.* only two. I wanted my nerves, my kidneys, and my eyes to function normally, to continue working much as they had up to then, for as long as possible. I decided to act on these results and change my insulin regimen at age 15.

Although problems with numbness, kidney failure, and vision typically do not show up for 10-  20 years after diabetes begins, they result from poor diabetic control over these intervening years. Both my doctor and Dad convinced me that the best treatment is prevention, which means good control today is necessary for good health in the future.

With Dr. Draznin's direction for better control of my disease, I switched to a combination of Ultralente® and Regular, stopping use of the intermediate-acting insulin NPH.

At first I was nervous about how I would manage taking three shots every day, but looking back, I am extremely happy I did it. Lo and behold, I regained a lot of my lost freedom with the new insulin regimen that also added to my responsibilities at the same time.

I needed to know how much insulin would match the amount of food I was going to eat. Learning to think like a pancreas was a small price to pay for recovering a lot of flexibility. As a high school student, I was involved in clubs, athletics, and many friendships.

Paw Paw *Courier-Leader* photo

My schedule was ever changing. With the rigidity of my former NPH and Regular regimen, it was difficult to manage with a variable activity schedule. As soon as I changed to a different insulin combination, I noticed immediate relief.

Look at school activities, for example. So I could have lunch timed correctly, changing my schedule used to mean switching out of classes I

wanted to take. Instead, with the new regimen, I took my insulin in class before lunch. Also, if I wanted to eat later than usual because of tennis practice or because I was going out to eat, I simply ate later and took my insulin just prior to eating— which became whenever I wanted.

Ultralente® made these freedoms possible by giving me an around-the-clock *basal insulin activity* without the need for a snack to avoid hypoglycemia.

This is the way it works:

- I take three shots a day, with Regular insulin in all of them. Each Regular shot covers the food I will eat right then for the next three to four hours.

- Two of these shots are mixed with Ultralente®. These are at breakfast and at dinner.

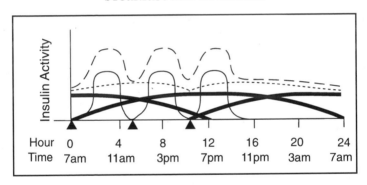

Hour	0	4	8	12	16	20	24
Time	7am	11am	3pm	7pm	11pm	3am	7am

▬▬▬ = Ultralente® insulin (three successive injections 10-12 hours apart)

——— = Regular insulin (three successive injections five to six hours apart)

- - - - - = Total Ultralente® insulin activity (the *combined* effect of three Ultralente® given at three different times about 12 hours apart). Note that the third injection hour (24) is the same as the first (0), and that total activity doesn't vary much.

— — — = Grand Total insulin activity. Note peaking hours during meal absorption times. However, they are a little delayed which requires waiting to eat after injection and/or snacking before the next meal.

▲ = Hour of Regular injection

= Hour of Ultralente® injection

- The Ultralente® supplies the body
  with a constant, slow-acting
  insulin, mimicking basal
  insulin activity which the
  body needs all the time (*see*
  graph, previous page). Since
  Ultralente® from dinner acts
  in you for so long, even if the
  Regular shot from dinner has
  all worn off, it is possible to
  sleep in late without having a
  morning high blood sugar.
- The amount of Regular insulin is
  determined by experience and
  with the help of your doctor
  or diabetes educator. This is
  taken only to cover the meal
  immediately ahead.

This new regimen also became very helpful
when different portions of food became a factor. If
I want a big breakfast, all I have to do is add a few
more units of Regular. If I want a smaller lunch
than usual, I merely take fewer units of Regular.

The new Ultralente®/Regular insulin regimen gave me these freedoms. I could not do this earlier. Both Regular and an intermediate-acting insulin, like NPH, in combination give a hard-to-calibrate, late insulin activity spurt, four to six hours after the injection that requires a lot of snacking.

Success with this regimen all depends on knowing what you want to eat, when you want to eat, and how much insulin to take for the amount of food you want to be eating.

NOTES

COMPLICATIONS AND RISK REDUCTION

Complications are other diseases or events related to a primary disease, such as diabetes. The complications that people with diabetes develop over the long term are nerve damage, kidney disease, and blindness. These conditions were studied for ten years by the National Institute of Diabetes and Digestive and Kidney Diseases. A Diabetes Control and Complications Trial Research Group (DCCT) report in the New England Journal of Medicine proved that intensive management of diabetes with insulin treatment slows, and may prevent, organ damage.

More frequent hypoglycemia was the only major drawback of intensive insulin therapy to ideally achieve less than 6% on a sugared hemoglobin blood test (HbA1c) in the

DCCT report. The recently completed Prospective Diabetes Study in the United Kingdom found that a one percent reduction in HbA1c produced a 25% decrease in diabetes-related death. Together, these studies point to HbA1c level over time as the strongest indicator of complication risk.

Diabetic Neuropathy

Recognition that diabetes caused nervous system diseases, what is now called *diabetic neuropathy,* first came to light in 1864. Nearly 70% of all diabetics suffer nerve damage. Most neurologic complications of diabetes involve the arms, feet, and legs, but medical researchers have yet to agree upon a single definition of diabetic neuropathy. European publications 100 years ago described it as follows:
- Numbness or tingling
- Loss of touch-pressure sensibility and tendon reflexes
- "Heavy legs"
- Foot ulcers
- Deep-seated ache in the marrow of the bones
- Great pain, particularly at night

Symptoms haven't changed. Proper foot care may help prevent amputation in later life. Diabetes can cause poor blood flow, thereby making wounds heal slowly or not at all. Free foot screening by podiatrists, under the sponsorship of the American Diabetes Association, discovered that 8% of people screened in Michigan pharmacies during 1998 required immediate attention.

Diabetic neuropathy can also lead to eye-muscle palsy, double vision, irregular digestion, and poor balance. Brain swelling is also possible because of coma (unconsciousness) induced by insulin shock or ketoacidosis. Its cause is still unknown. Neuropathy may occur because sorbitol is deposited in the nerves ten years after diabetic diagnosis. Approved treatment is pain management and close control of high blood sugar, which the DCCT showed reduced the nephropathy risk by 60%.

Diabetic Nephropathy

We depend on our kidneys to filter excessive substances from our blood in the process of producing urine and excreting it from our bodies. Nephropathy is caused by damage to the small blood vessels in the kidney or to the kidney's blood-cleaning cells (glomeruli) which then do not filter wastes from the blood. Most studies of *diabetic nephropathy* have been done on Type I diabetes. It is a serious problem that requires laboratory testing to confirm.

Diabetic nephropathy occurs when more than 0.5g protein is present in the urine (proteinuria) over 24 hours. Retinopathy and high blood pressure also support this complication. Over time actual kidney failure develops which requires machine dialysis or a kidney transplant.

Diabetes mellitus is the most common cause of end-stage renal disease in the U.S. About 10% more blood plasma flows through the kidneys of insulin-dependent diabetics than normal. A chronic breakdown occurs when nitrogenous wastes build up in blood plasma from abnormal metabolism of protein, for example, or when the kidneys fail to regulate the volume or composition of fluids bathing its cells. Chronic renal failure (CRF) is generally irreversible and progressive in nature.

CRF develops insidiously and only when the glomeruli lose 70% of their normal filtration capacity. This condition can be indicated by complaints of fatigue, sleep disturbances, nausea and vomiting, or severe itching of otherwise undamaged skin. Often patients don't know they have it until tests show that urea and creatinine, which are nitrogen-containing end products of protein metabolism usually found in urine, are also found in blood. Because blood in urine usually precedes development of CRF, urinalysis remains an important screening test for patients during periodic health evaluations.

Half of all diabetes patients develop kidney disease. More men than women develop proteinuria and diabetic retinopathy. Type I patients show protein in their urine after 10-20 years of diabetes, followed by two to three years of progressive renal insufficiency. Urine dipsticks are now available that can detect extremely small amounts of albumin, typical of this stage. This suggests a likely progression to CRF in five years. If microalbumin values are 30µ-200µ, eating less protein and taking modern medication may reverse or slow down nephropathy. Intensive blood sugar control with insulin, to maintain close to normal range levels, delays onset and slows progression of diabetic nephropathy. It reduces the risk of this complication by 50%.

Diabetic Retinopathy

Diabetic retinopathy is the leading cause of blindness among Americans 21-74 years old, many of whom have no warning. It occurs progressively, beginning with damaged blood vessels that leak in the back of the eye. Their bleeding first blurs, then blocks, vision. Further impaired vision and finally blindness occur when scar tissue forms from these tiny broken blood vessels *(capillaries)* to pull the retina away from the back of the eye.

> "Control of blood sugar reduced the risk of eye disease by 76%."

Lack of enough insulin itself can cause diabetic retinopathy. High blood sugar levels occur with, and probably cause, changes in eye structures and functions. They also prompt changes in hormones that cause loss of function in capillaries of the retina. These capillary injuries, if found when they've just begun, can be halted by laser treatments which prevent retinal detachment. Identifying eyes at risk and referring patients to laser surgery is the physician's goal. The recommended time for Type I patients to get their first eye exam is five years after diabetes onset or during puberty, with yearly follow up.

Even though recent publications tell us that diabetic retinopathy is neither preventable nor curable, researchers point to the DCCT study which determined that very tight control of blood glucose levels reduces the risk of renal and retinal complications of diabetes. Control of blood sugar reduced the eye disease risk by 76% and can reduce the five-year risk of developing this complication to less than 5%. Until retinopathy can be prevented or cured, careful follow up once it's identified is warranted.

Risk reduction of both medical and social complications goes with good blood sugar control. Upon diagnosis, drivers with diabetes in Minnesota must notify its Department of Public Safety's Driver and Vehicle Services Division (DVSD). If a hypoglycemic event leads to a traffic accident, the driver's license is suspended. A physician's signature, certifying that the driver's blood sugar is in good control, must accompany a driver's license reapplication form to reinstate driving privileges.

INSULIN TIMING

Regular insulin begins to be effective 30-45 minutes after injection. It reaches its maximum activity at two to four hours, and it stops acting about five hours after injection.

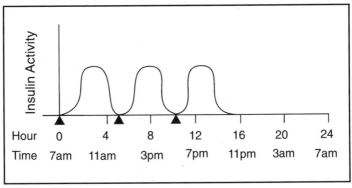

————— = Regular insulin (three successive injections)
▲ = Hour of injection

This activity schedule is fine, if you have time to inject a full half hour before a meal and the meal is big

71

enough, and of such a nature, that it will be absorbed over a two- to four-hour span to match Regular insulin activity. However, the Regular insulin is far from ideal if any of these conditions occur:

- There is not enough time to inject a full half-hour before the meal,
- A meal is not of such a nature that it will have a prolonged absorption process, or
- Athletic activity is going to take place after a meal, while the insulin activity is still happening

What is needed under these circumstances is a quicker, shorter-acting insulin.

Basal Insulin Activity

When a normal body is at rest, its pancreas produces a continuous supply of insulin at very low levels, about 1 mg (25-30 units) of insulin per day, known as its *basal insulin activity.* Some diabetics who take their medication in programmed insulin doses with pump therapy match this rate.

Regular insulin is used to mimic the normal process for the immediate needs of the body when a meal is being absorbed. However, a longer-acting insulin is needed to cover those times when you are not eating because the body has a basal insulin need all the time, whether you are absorbing food or not. NPH was developed for this reason. NPH insulin becomes effective about four hours after injections, reaches its maximum activity at six to eight hours after injection, and stops acting ten to twelve hours after injection. NPH is longer acting than Regular because of the added protein, protamine.

NPH is fine if you are able to follow its schedule rigidly. This means meals and snacks eaten at the same time every day and athletic activity participation is done on a rigid time schedule. However, if you cannot adhere to this schedule, or you would like the freedom from such a schedule,

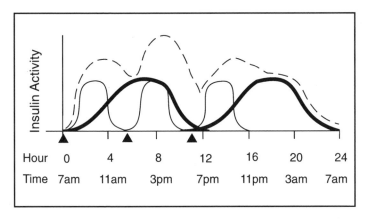

━━━ = NPH insulin (two successive injections)
───── = Regular insulin (three successive injections)
─ ─ ─ = Grand Total insulin activity. Note late morning and mid-
    afternoon peaks that require snacking. Also note
    minimal basal levels of insulin activity in the several
    hours before waking that results in hyperglycemia
    upon arising.
▲ = Hour of Regular injection
   = Hour of NPH injection

then NPH will not work well. What is needed in these circumstances is a long-acting insulin with a low enough activity
peak such that it does not produce hypoglycemia requiring a
corrective snack.

For teens learning to adjust their insulin dosages,
change slowly—only one type of insulin at a time. It may
take two or three days after insulin is adjusted to notice
changes in patterns of high or low blood glucose.

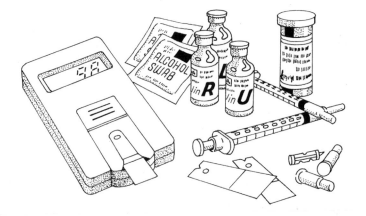

Chapter 8

Athletics

Being involved in an active event can at first be very intimidating to a person with diabetes. My activities included varsity sports such as basketball, tennis, and golf, as well as indoor soccer and some jogging.

For regulating my diabetes during athletics, the most important thing that I had to remember was the idea of using an intelligent trial and error process. Every diabetic patient knows that it is impossible to get perfect control the first time doing something new, but that does not mean it cannot happen. It is imperative that you learn from your experiences. For instance, when I was playing basketball, I burned a lot of calories. If I ate nothing prior to a practice or game, I was sure to go "low."

Therefore, eating a sandwich beforehand with two starches and one to two meats gave me enough energy, most of the time (but not always), for roughly two hours of hard activity. However, sometimes I would be "high" when I tested at half-time, about 220 to 260 mg/dl. After review I discovered that swigs of sugared sport drinks put my blood sugar high if I had already eaten a sandwich.

Rarely did I have to inject insulin for these pre-athletic snacks because the morning Ultralente® and residual Regular insulin activity from lunch or dinner were still present when the events took place. Although my blood sugar was high one day, I did not drastically change anything the next day; otherwise I would likely have had a big low. Instead, I slowly worked out the problem by changing only one factor, such as the amount of protein, by a modest amount one day at a time. By the middle of the season my basketball regimen had all the kinks worked out.

It is also important to know that when you eat a pre-exercise snack, timing makes a difference. If you eat too early, you may end up being high before the event and then have the snack's effect wear off before the event is completed, leaving you low. On the other hand if you eat right before, the "carbos" might kick in just before the end of the activity. You will then have extra unburned calories still being absorbed into your bloodstream, leaving you way too high.

Since it is usually necessary for people with diabetes to eat before an athletic activity, upset stomachs are quite possible. To prevent this, here are a few helpful hints to aid digestion:

1. Sports drinks with sugar are good for combating lows with quick energy.

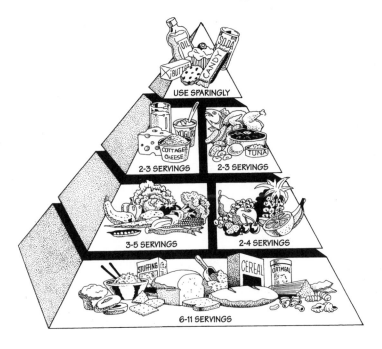

2. Foods high in complex carbohydrates are good for sustaining a good blood sugar level for a long period of time.

3. Chew the food well.

4. Eat the food slowly.

5. Avoid greasy or very spicy foods.

In the beginning, just after learning that
you are insulin dependent, it is important to test
your blood level before and after every activity.
Later on, test occasionally to be sure your body is
still responding as expected. With time, after trial
and error, each person finds his or her own best
time and best snack prior to athletic activities.

NOTES

COMPLEX CARBOHYDRATES

Starches in grains and vegetables consist of *complex carbohydrates* like galactosides and cellulose. Digestive juices all along the digestive tract either sequentially break down these starches into secondary and simple sugars or eliminate their insoluble and indigestible parts in feces.

The USDA recommends that 55-60% of daily calories come from starches in 6-11 servings of grain-rich breads, cereals, rice, and pasta. Fewer servings (1-2) of starchy vegetables (legumes and roots), like beans, peas, potatoes, carrots, and turnips, go into a well-balanced diet and also leave room everyday for 2-3 servings of leafy vegetables.

Since each food category (simple or complex carbohydrates, proteins, and fat) metabolizes at different rates, and since we need to have something (kicking in) at all times, eating something from each category will give the most consistent delivery of glucose to the bloodstream. A peanut butter sandwich has simple carbs in the jelly, complex carbs in the bread, and protein and fat in the peanut butter. Simple carbs take little processing by the body and will kick in quickly, maybe 5-15 minutes after eating. Simple sugar starts and dissipates quickly. Complex carbs take about 10-25 minutes; protein, 30 minutes; and fat, two hours. Fat not only takes a long time to kick in but also stays around the longest.

FOOD EXCHANGES

Healthy diets for diabetics and non-diabetics alike contain a balance of nutrients. Exchange lists were developed to maintain balance. They group foods by type and serving size. Within each food group on these lists, each serving has about the same amount of carbohydrates, protein, fat, and calories:

- Starch/Bread
- Vegetable
- Fruit
- Milk
- Meat
- Fat

While your life-style sets the numbers of calories and exchanges in your diet, foods within a food group can be exchanged or substituted with another food serving in the same group. *See* next page for a sample exchange list.

Note that both the milk and meat groups can have smaller subgroups according to their fat content (low, medium, high). While all foods in the meat group, for example, have 7 g protein in one serving, the amount of fat varies from 3 g (low fat) and 5 g (medium), to 8 g (high) per serving. The more fat, the higher the calories. Just remember that unsaturated vegetable fats produce lower blood cholesterol than saturated animal fats.

A Sample Exchange List

Group	Food Choices	Serving Size
Starch	Bran flakes cereal	1/2 cup
	Saltine crackers	6 squares
	Whole wheat bread	1 slice
	Corn on the cob	6 inches
	Potato chips	10-15 chips
Vegetable	Broccoli	All types:
	Carrots	1/2 cup cooked
	Mushrooms	or
	Tomato	1 cup raw
Fruit	Apple	1
	Banana	1/2
	Strawberries	1-1/2 cup
	Grapefruit juice	1/2 cup
Milk*	Milk (L,M,H)	1 cup
	Yogurt (L,M,H)	1 cup
Meat*	Pork chop (M)	1 oz
	Hamburger (H)	1 oz
	Boiled ham (L)	1 oz
	Chicken (L,M)	1 oz
	Egg whites (L)	3
	Shrimp (L)	2 oz
	Tuna (L,M)	1/4 cup
	Cottage cheese (L)	1/4 cup
	Mozzarella cheese (M)	1 oz
	Cheddar cheese (H)	1 oz
Fat*	Butter (S)	1 teaspoon
	Margarine (U)	1 teaspoon
	Salad dressing (U)	1 Tablespoon
	Bacon (S)	1 slice
	Cream cheese (S)	1 Tablespoon
	Peanuts (U)	15

*Fat content: H=high, L=low, M=medium
S=saturated, U=unsaturated

81

High blood cholesterol may be lowered by diet, exercise, and medication. Eating less animal fat and more polyunsaturated fats from fish and vegetables, like avocados and nuts, produces good blood:fat ratios regardless of eating cholesterol-rich foods like eggs. Dietary fat is necessary and particularly important during periods of fasting, such as overnight, when it is very slowly absorbed.

Athletes who want to build muscle should not consume protein supplements, but plan weight-resistant exercise instead. Getting in shape is hard work; there are no short cuts. Avoid too much protein in your blood to ease kidney function, with safety as a priority. Excess protein and kidneys of people with diabetes is a bad combination.

EXERCISE AND STRESS

The relationship between food and insulin is like that between stress and exercise; as the first builds up, the second breaks it down. Some people deal with stress by

eating "comfort foods." Eating carbohydrate-rich foods and cutting back on protein, such as meat and eggs, may help people deal with stress. Carbohydrates increase the amount of serotonin in the brain that prevents stressful feelings, and exercise increases the body's sensitivity to insulin. The more we exercise, the less insulin we may need to take because our cells have developed more receptors that use insulin more efficiently.

Exercise is the only known way to increase the number of insulin receptors on a human cell. Everyone benefits from regular exercise chosen because it is enjoyable. For instance, walking and running are both good exercise for maintaining normal foot circulation as much in non-athletic diabetics as anyone else. You can change diabetes management to fit the kind of exercise you like best. You don't have to change your exercise to fit diabetes. It's all a matter of thinking ahead.

As long as urine ketones are *not* present, exercising effectively lowers high blood sugar. However, during the first hour of exercise, blood sugars may actually increase slightly because of the body's release of adrenaline which prompts the break down of glycogen, the starch stored in muscles, into sugar for energy. Blood sugar may then decline and continue to do so for up to 12 hours after exercise because sugar is taken from the blood to replace the muscle carbohydrate used during exercise.

Because more activity and excitement burn more sugar, less insulin is needed during exercise periods. When you visit your doctor or diabetes educator, discuss how to regulate the insulin you need during exercise.

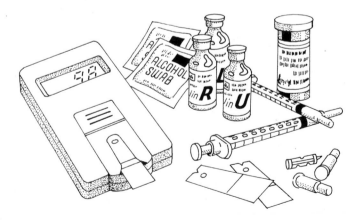

Chapter 9

A Handy New Tool

My diabetes control had gotten very tight,
except for a few situations. For instance, in the
morning I would take my Ultralente® and Regular
insulins, and at lunch time my blood sugar would
be fine. However, when I checked it at 9:00 a.m.,
two hours after eating, I found that it was around
230 mg/dl.

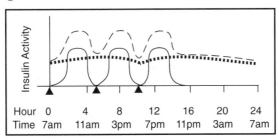

Hour   0   4   8   12   16   20   24
Time 7am   11am   3pm   7pm   11pm   3am   7am

———   = Regular insulin
■ ■ ■ = Total Ultralente® insulin activity
– – – = Grand Total insulin activity
▲ = Hour of Regular injection
   = Hour of Ultralente® injection

85

Adding more Regular at breakfast to get my after-breakfast reading lower was a problem because then I would be very low for lunch (*see* table, page 92). To compensate for this, I always had to have a bigger, more filling snack than usual at about 10:00 a.m. That worked, but I did not always like to have to eat a sandwich or comparable amount of food mid-morning every day, especially during my classes.

Then Humalog® became available my junior year. This was a perfect solution. It takes effect much more quickly than Regular. Instead of having to wait thirty minutes before eating with Regular, I only had to wait about ten minutes. But the real advantage came with how quickly it is in and out of your system.

Humalog® activity peaks at about one hour after injection, whereas Regular peaks between two and four hours. What this means is that while your breakfast food is being absorbed, the insulin activity of Humalog® is acting simultaneously. In

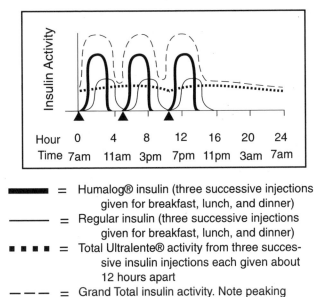

■■■■■■ = Humalog® insulin (three successive injections given for breakfast, lunch, and dinner)

───── = Regular insulin (three successive injections given for breakfast, lunch, and dinner)

■ ■ ■ ■ = Total Ultralente® activity from three successive insulin injections each given about 12 hours apart

─ ─ ─ = Grand Total insulin activity. Note peaking occurs during meal absorption *without* delay, thus avoiding having to wait to eat and/or snack before the next meal.

▲ = Hour of Humalog® and Regular injection

= Hour of Ultralente® injection

short, a snack is not needed and should not be taken.

The reason you eat a snack with Regular is because it peaks two to four hours after injection and your meal. You want to have carbohydrates being absorbed in your intestine when Regular insulin is peaking. Humalog® offers activity peaks simultaneously with food from a meal being digested and absorbed, but no longer than your body takes for these tasks. If you were to eat a snack later on while on Humalog®, since there is

> **"Humalog® gives you a great deal of freedom."**

little insulin activity left by then, your blood sugar would most likely run quite high before your next meal and injection.

Remember this: repeated bouts of hyperglycemia that keep blood glucose continuously above normal lead to long-term complications of diabetic neuropathy, nephropathy, and retinopathy with your nerves, kidneys, and eyes. Be careful, and don't overcompensate. Although maintaining normal blood sugar is the goal of diabetes care, doing it safely while avoiding severe lows is still an art.

So, Humalog® gives you a great deal of freedom. When planning an activity, you do not have to plan a snack and its necessary interruption. When you are in a restaurant, you do not need to guess when the food will be ready; about ten minutes or less is all you need to wait. Most importantly, Humalog® lowers or eliminates the high post-meal blood sugars without making you low before your next meal.

NOTES

PRE-MEAL TESTS

Scenario

You check your blood sugar before bedtime. It is normal, so you eat a normal snack because your Regular

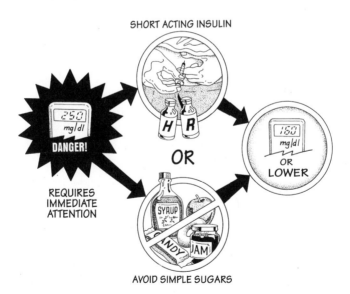

SHORT ACTING INSULIN

DANGER!

REQUIRES
IMMEDIATE
ATTENTION

OR

AVOID SIMPLE SUGARS

insulin is still active. Then in the morning before breakfast, you check again, fully expecting it to be normal. However, instead you test at 250 mg/dl, and you do not know what happened.

A high pre-meal test can a result from several factors, either from just one or from a combination of many as shown in the accompanying table (*see* next page). These same reasons apply to any high blood sugar, and the higher the reading merely suggests that the already mentioned factors may be manifesting themselves more strongly or have been happening for longer periods of time. A blood sugar of 160 mg/dl can result for the same reason as a 240 or even 400 mg/dl. These highs usually mean that it has gone undetected and uncorrected for an even longer time.

Perhaps you had too much snack at bedtime on top of a big dinner or maybe an illness started and overnight basal insulin activity may have changed? Particularly in the morning, your adrenal glands could have released a normal amount of cortisol and other steroids that take sugar from your liver and put it into your bloodstream. You may be under more stress than usual.

Ways to Combat Pre-Meal Highs

Immediate Attention

No matter what the reason, blood glucose of 250 mg/dl needs to be taken care of right away with short-acting insulin and a urine check for ketones. Here are actions for that day:
- Take more than the usual amount of short-acting insulin before the meal
- Take short-acting insulin and wait longer before eating
- Both of the above, or
- Change your diet to avoid simple sugars in meals

After taking one of these steps, be sure to check your blood sugar after the meal to see whether or not the method you chose put you back into the normal range.

While the pre-meal chart on the next page works for me, it might not be exactly like the one you develop for

Pre-Meal Blood Tests

Blood Sugar Level	Test Result	Intrepretation	Reasons for These Levels
Over 240 mg/dl	Very HIGH	Needs **attention** *now*	Overused injection site unable to process insulin as usual Infection
240-160 mg/dl	HIGH	Needs attention	Illness Insulin no longer good, possibly outdated or kept too warm
160-120 mg/dl	Slightly HIGH	Needs fine tuning	Ate too soon after taking insulin More stress than usual, requiring more basal insulin Too much food* for the amount of insulin at the previous meal Less activity* after previous meal than planned or needed
120-80 mg/dl	*NORMAL*	*Ideal*	*Correct balance of insulin, diet, exercise, stress, etc., since your last meal*
80-60 mg/dl	LOW	Needs attention	Too much insulin from previous meal Not enough or right kinds of food More physical activity than planned since previous meal

* Most likely factors.

yourself. Blood sugar levels above 60 mg/dl are okay on most meters because they usually measure whole blood, not plasma, levels. Health care professionals are likely to use a broader "ideal" target of 70-150 mg/dl for pre-meal tests. The reasons I've given to explain various levels are reasonable, but your body reactions may differ enough from mine so that all of them won't apply to you. Work with your health care team to personalize your diabetes management.

Sometimes Dr. Draznin and my health care team, for instance, have used a "supplement scale" with adolescents when their pre-meal glucose tests register above 150 mg/dl. This scale calls for an additional unit of short-acting insulin for each 50 mg/dl above the 150 trigger. His team also teaches "pattern recognition skills" to catch persistent high or low readings over several days at any pre-meal or bedtime tests. These would lead to a change in the base dose of insulin.

Future Attention

To prevent problems in the future—as best you can—be sure to **stop and think** about what might have caused your blood sugar to be higher at that time, for example:
- If you ate too much (something easily accounted for), then either eat the correct amount the next day or take more short-acting insulin to cover it.
- If your eating habits were normal, it is possible that your basal insulin requirements have risen. Therefore, add some more units of long-acting insulin, with experimentation in mind.

However, maybe doing these things doesn't seem to help and you really may be sick. Okay, it's time to contact your doctor, describe your "high" and how you tried to bring it down, and ask what you need to do instead.

Chapter 10

Fine Tuning for the Long Haul

Once I had the basic knowledge and understanding of diabetes, and a decent comprehension
of regulation, I decided there were a few things I
could do either more practically or in a more
beneficial manner. This was not to say that my
control was bad, but I was now preparing myself
for the long road of lifetime control. What system
could I find that would be acceptable until the
time research makes its next breakthrough available for use?

Up until age 17, as a senior in high school, I
had been eating peanut butter on toast every
morning to let my bloodstream absorb the sugar in

my breakfast at a slower and steadier rate than what would certainly occur with a mostly carbohydrate meal. Peanut butter has a high fat content which slows the digestion and absorption of

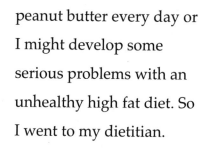

carbohydrate. This worked, but I realized I would not be able to eat peanut butter every day or I might develop some serious problems with an unhealthy high fat diet. So I went to my dietitian.

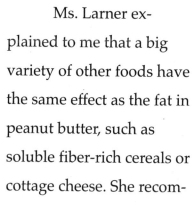

Ms. Larner explained to me that a big variety of other foods have the same effect as the fat in peanut butter, such as soluble fiber-rich cereals or cottage cheese. She recommended I switch to these other foods often. My diet became healthier and less monotonous.

Let your dietitian help with your blood sugar control and enjoyment of eating. Be pre-

pared for those office visits with specific food and
control questions, like these:

- What are examples of foods whose carbohydrates are absorbed quickly?
- What foods added to a meal slow down
and even out the absorption of
carbohydrates?
- What meal preparation methods affect
absorption?

Trusting your dietitian's answers, and then actually using them, can make life a lot better for you.

Also, I found that with
Humalog®, often it is not necessary to eat extra protein/fat foods
to slow the absorption of sugar
because short-acting Humalog®
may be out of your system before
the carbohydrate mixed with
protein and fat kick in.

Another fine tuning I did had to do with
my injection-site rotation. I sketched a map of my
own body and all of its possible injection sites,

keeping about an inch or an inch and a half between adjacent sites. Then, as I used one site, I

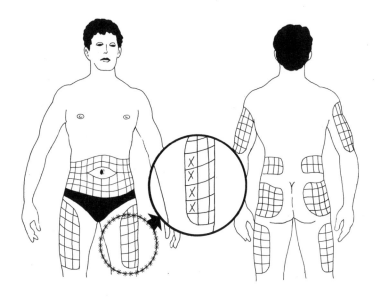

would simply cross it off on my paper map. Although I am not an artist, it didn't matter. My map
was clear enough for me to follow. Once I had
used all the sites, I would start over and repeat the
pattern.

It is extremely important to rotate insulin
injection sites to keep them functioning properly
all life long. Sites used too frequently or with too
rapid injection of the insulin become scarred

under the skin. Then insulin absorption rates become unpredictable, either too fast or too slow.

Given the consequences, I not only drew a personal map of possible injection sites and used it systematically to rotate my injections, but committed it to memory. Now I simply follow my own map mentally.

NOTES

INJECTION-SITE ROTATION

Rotating locations for giving yourself insulin injections will keep lumps or small dents, called *lipodystrophies*, from forming in the skin. These uneven dimples look like the popular cosmetic nemesis, cellulite!

Even though you rotate your injection sites, try to use the same body area for injections given at the same time each day. For example, you might use your stomach area each morning and an arm in the afternoon or evening. This kind of routine lessens the possibility of changes in the timing and action of whatever insulin you inject.

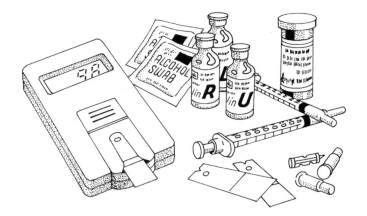

Chapter 11

Finer Tuning

When you get to a stage in your diabetic control where your pre-meal and other scheduled blood sugar testing results are at desired levels,

then you have achieved a most difficult goal. You can be very proud of this achievement. However, circumstances are always changing, whether or not you are aware of it, even though you think

99

things are fine, they still might be improved. Maintaining good health is your responsibility.

Blood sugar levels can fluctuate significantly within a period of time from the pre-meal injection to the end of the insulin activity, and for this reason it is imperative to occasionally check

Desired Glucometer Readings

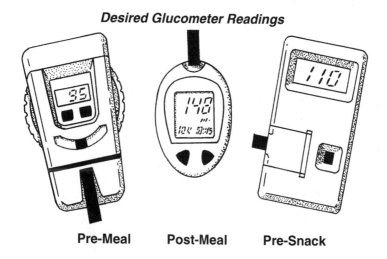

| Pre-Meal | Post-Meal | Pre-Snack |

your blood sugar level between the pre-injection check and the pre-snack or next meal test, preferably about two hours after eating.

Often, the blood sugar is normal before a meal, rises too high directly after the meal, then goes right down to normal once the insulin starts peaking while you are doing your pre-snack test. This gives you a normal reading, but not normal blood sugar levels in that duration of time.

To safeguard against post-meal highs, it is necessary to check your blood sugar occasionally after meals. When you have achieved normal readings at all three testing times—pre-meal, post-meal, and pre-next meal—you should continue the practice once or twice a month.

Post-Meal Tests

A good thing to do when checking after a meal is to account for all the factors that affect your blood sugar. Consider how each had affected you that day, and then try to guess what your blood sugar will be before the glucometer gives a reading. This exercise will help you to physically "Know thyself." It's one way of learning how to think like a pancreas.

For example, if you eat a normal meal for that particular time and do more sitting around than usual, but took the usual dose of insulin, you might guess that your blood sugar will be a little higher than normal (maybe something between 160 and 180 mg/dl). Once you get an actual result from your glucometer, do not just read it. Assess it immediately for what it means by asking yourself, "What factors contributed to the high, low, or normal reading?"

If the glucometer reading is not where you want it, take the necessary actions to get it there. This is how you learn "finer tuning."

For instance, you might have expected your blood sugar to be between 160 and 180 mg/dl, but instead the actual reading was 270 mg/dl. You probably needed more Humalog® or Regular insulin for that set of circumstances. If it was 70 mg/dl, then you probably needed less short-acting insulin, more food, or a combination of those two factors.

Insulin Combinations

I found a way to get my post-meal test into an even tighter range. A handy tool is the triple combination of Humalog®, Regular, and Ultralente® insulins all in one injection. This is done by drawing two types of insulin into one syringe and merely adding one more type.

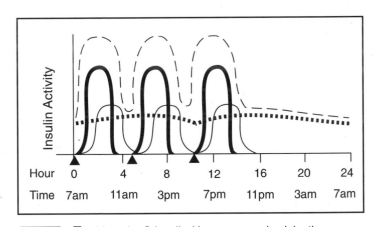

▬▬▬	=	Humalog® insulin (three successive injections before meals)
———	=	Regular insulin (three successive injections before meals)
▪ ▪ ▪ ▪	=	Total Ultralente® insulin activity (three successive injections about 12 hours apart)
— ——	=	Grand Total insulin activity
▲	=	Hour of injection

I start with Humalog®, then add Regular, and end with Ultralente®. The Humalog® can cover quickly absorbed carbohydrates in pre-sugars and fruits, while Regular covers the later absorbing foods, such as complex carbohydrates mixed with proteins and fats (*see* Notes in previous chapters). Finally, Ultralente® continues to cover the basal insulin requirements of your body. These three categories of insulin needs match up very nicely with these three insulin types.

Be aware, however, that using this triple combination method can make success more difficult to achieve. Nevertheless, as you apply an intelligent trial-and-error process, the likely good results will be much better than the double combination used previously.

Check with your doctor before doing this because it has not been reviewed by the FDA. Although your doctor may allow you to do this, the insulin manufacturing company has not yet recommended it. On the other hand, your doctor may not want you to try this for reasons he or she will certainly explain to you. Even my doctor

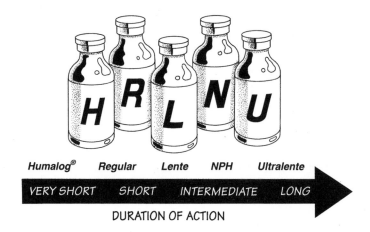

Humalog®   Regular   Lente   NPH   Ultralente

VERY SHORT   SHORT   INTERMEDIATE   LONG

DURATION OF ACTION

would not advocate this plan for others since it really hasn't been studied.

The type of insulin regimen described above is extremely helpful in certain special situations. If you are a student, for example, with classes in the afternoon that do not allow you to burn a lot of calories and at the same time give you some stress, you may want a good-sized lunch to prepare for a long afternoon. Here the combination of Regular and Humalog® can be very helpful.

Humalog® provides full coverage of the meal without fear of late lows. If you were to take just Humalog®, the slower absorbing foods from lunch would not get insulin coverage, causing your post-meal blood sugar to be normal, but your pre-dinner reading to be high. On the other hand, if you were to take just Regular, your pre-dinner reading would be fine, but you would probably discover your post-meal check to be high because Regular is a slower-acting insulin.

With both kinds of short-acting insulin, potentially each of your post-meal and pre-dinner readings can be normal. Even in people without diabetes, circulating insulin following a meal rises five to ten-fold and then gradually declines to basal levels as insulin is cleared from circulation.

NOTES

FDA

Within the executive branch of U.S. government is the Department of Health and Human Services (HHS). The U.S. Food and Drug Administration (FDA) within HHS is a regulatory agency with a 20th century history beginning in 1938 when congress gave it authority over the Food, Drug, and Cosmetic Act.

The FDA regulates prescription and non-prescription drugs to insure their safety and effectiveness for both humans and animals. Medical devices, radiation-emitting consumer products, food additives, and cosmetics also fall within its regulatory responsibility. FDA monitors the manufacture, import, transport, storage, and sale of $1,000,000,000,000 worth of goods annually.

Pharmaceutical companies are required by the FDA to show that a medication works safely. Initial animal testing data for a particular drug are compiled as an Investigative New Drug (IND) document. After FDA approval of the IND, companies proceed with testing in humans, first for safety in small studies, then for effectiveness in larger clinical trials. Personnel within the FDA oversee and communicate directly with drug company representatives throughout this process to help shape the resulting New Drug Application (NDA). Companies must report unexpected serious adverse effects on an ongoing basis once they learn of them. Final approval for manufacture, sale, and use of new drugs for particular indications by FDA scientists usually comes after thorough review by a panel of experts.

If you experience a bad reaction to any medication, contact your doctor right away. If your reaction is unusual or unexpected, your doctor may report it to the drug company or to the FDA. However, since the FDA does not require health care professionals to report these problems, you may contact the agency by letter or phone:
U.S. Food and Drug Administration
5600 Fishers Lane
Rockville, MD 20857
1-301-827-2410

The FDA maintains a website (http://www.fda.gov) on which it posts revisions of its rules and transcripts of its hearings. In March 1998, it led a discussion of issues surrounding self-monitoring of blood glucose (SMBG) systems, glucose meters, and test strips. This SMBG discussion intended to clarify realistic expectations about these devices, based on current technology for doctors and patients. You can read the transcript online.

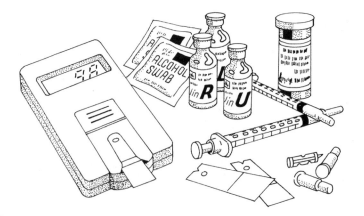

Chapter 12

A Visit to My Doctor

A routine visit to a doctor's office can be a nervous, even scary, experience. Facing older people, the high-tech equipment, and the fact that you are at the center of it all, can be enough to overwhelm anyone. However, find the pattern in these appoint-ments and real-ize that the  doctor's team is there to help, not merely to see you. The whole trip can be quite informative, very worthwhile, and even fun. Yes!

For me, a typical visit to the doctor's office consists of meeting with four people, who have focused their attention on different aspects of me and my health, to review their findings. Each medical staff person should give me the opportunity to ask any and as many questions as I wish. If they cannot answer them right then, they should—and do—get back to me as soon as possible. Because these questions are so important, I plan ahead and come up with a list of all my questions, usually several, before I go in for my appointment. These vary from simple yes or no questions to ones that need more complex answers.

These people should be consulted for different reasons when you visit your doctor:
- Nurse—tests and questions
- Dietitian—diet and insulin reactions
- Diabetes educator, who may also be a nurse —technological advances and amount of insulin I take
- Doctor—partial physical and getting to know one another

You may visit people on your health care team in a different order than I do, but it is essential that all of them are available.

First I see Michael McCarthy, the nurse who does all the statistical tests on me. These include checking and recording my height and weight, pulse rate, and blood pressure. He also takes a urine sample and checks my glucometer against his. Do they give the same readings? These meters cannot be adjusted. When they become inaccurate, we throw them out and buy new ones.

Of course, my nurse answers my questions, which is the most important of his tasks. For example, I have asked him to recommend the best, most economical way to purchase supplies. Sometimes I wanted to know what certain test results mean and how I could make them better.

Next the dietitian, another key person in my trip to the doctor's office, speaks with me. We discuss questions about diet, food value or content, meal planning, and handling insulin reactions, all of which are necessary and should be taken seriously.

Just before seeing the doctor, I talk with a diabetes educator who is knowledgeable about new advances in the technology of diabetes care. We discuss what is and what is not working for me. It is imperative that I am open and honest with her about many things. These points are particularly crucial:

- the amount of insulin I am taking,
- what my blood sugar readings are, and
- whether there may be times of day I have difficulty stabilizing my blood sugar.

I take these topics very seriously because they are key to the effectiveness of my office visit.

Finally, here comes the doctor. It can be tempting not to ask him many questions, now that I have talked so much with everyone else. However, he is the person who can and should give me the most information.

As my doctor does a partial physical, checking such things as my eyes, lungs, and muscles,

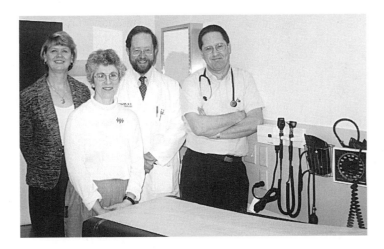

we usually talk informally with each other. These chats have allowed us to get to know each other on a personal level, and I have become more comfortable talking about diabetes with him because of them. In other words, since the most important parts of a doctor's office visit are asking questions and learning, I have found that getting

to really know the doctor makes this important process easier.

After I meet with my diabetes team, I get my blood drawn to give my doctor and me a better understanding of how my body is being affected by diabetes on a long-term basis. During every visit to his office, usually every three months, I have a urine sample tested for proteins and a blood sample tested for hemoglobin A1c on the chance that they will signal bad news. My HbA1c informs us of my body's average blood sugar level over the past three months. High blood sugar and high blood pressure push some blood proteins into urine, creating damaged kidneys.

These tests are an extremely crucial element of my checkups, each and every time. I want to know enough to stay healthy.

Knowing my hemoglobin A1c is essential because it allows me to learn what my blood sugar levels have been doing throughout all 24 hours of the day, whereas the finger-stick blood check gives me a reading at one particular moment. Finger-stick checks do not show possible high fluctuations in my glucose levels. I do not mean to suggest that they are not important; they give me the information I need to reduce the number of fluctuations that may occur.

Once a year my blood is tested for other factors in addition to my hemoglobin A1c. Testing for total cholesterol, HDL and LDL cholesterols, and thyroxine hormone adds to laboratory data useful to my continued health (*see* Afterword). At my next visit, my doctor discusses the results of these tests with me, either in person or occasionally in a letter. Be sure to have your doctor explain and discuss your results with you.

Making best use of your doctor's office visits requires some preparation on your part:

- Go with a few already written questions.
- Know what to expect.
- Expect to learn from the whole medical staff.
- Do not be afraid.

After all, your doctor and his trained associates are there to help YOU.

Chapter 13

Getting On With My Life

When I took over my diabetes control on September 28, 1993, I had no idea of what to expect. I was completely ignorant of the disease, I felt like I was in way over my head, and I was scared. Not long after, however, I realized that I enjoyed doing so much prior to the time diabetes became a part of my life. Why should that change?

I still wanted to do everything done in the past and probably try new things, too. By choice, I decided this disease was not going to stop me.

There was a lot to learn to continue being able to enjoy my normally active life-style. I am

Kalamazoo *Gazette*, Paw Paw *Courier-Leader*, VBYC, and Melluish family photos

still learning today, along with my doctors, nurses, diabetic educators, and dietitians.

All of the knowledge I accumulated since my diagnosis has allowed me to get on with my life, one step at a time. Instead of leaving it all to my parents, who have encouraged and supported my independence, I feel in complete control of managing my diabetes.

Petoskey *News-Review, VBYC,* and Melluish family photos

Taking back my life has meant learning to ask questions that doctors are not accustomed to answering and developing high expectations about self-regulation. The keys to looking beyond diabetes were setting my own goals and accomplishing them myself.

I still involve myself in many activities, studies, clubs, social events, athletics, and everything else that non-diabetics can do. Most of the time, my involvement is without worry. Now I even view my diabetes as a unique character trait—something to set me apart from so many others. We diabetics share this trait.

> **"I still [do]... everything ...that non-diabetics can do."**

Diabetes is a disease that has the potential to hinder us, but we do not have to allow that consequence. I am going to continue living my healthful life with freedom, and so can you.

Afterword

Okay, we have done a lot so far:

- Found out our pancreas doesn't work

- Learned to think like a pancreas

- Figured out how to test and eat and act and then test some more

- Taught our school teachers and staff real lessons in continuing education, and

- Given our parents more material for family stories about what makes us unique people

So now what? Is there any more to know? I hope the details included in this Afterword suggest we can always learn more.

WORD CONSTRUCTION

Medical and chemical terms often come from classical language roots. From Latin comes neuro-, renes, and retino- for nerve, renal/kidneys, and retina. We take nephro- and -patho- from Greek for kidney and for suffering or disease, respectively. Greek is also the source for the majority of specialized words used in this book. The short table below gives a few examples:

Greek roots or stems	English meanings
-ase	enzyme
chroma-	color
dys-	bad, difficult, or impaired
-gen	producer
-globin	protein
gluco-	sugar
glyc-	sugar
hemo-	blood
hyper-	above or beyond
hypo-	under, down, or beneath
lipo-	fat or fatty
-meter	measure
mono-	one or single
-ol	alcohol
-ose	sugar
poly-	many
sacchar-	sugar
troph-	turn towards or nuture

MORE ON CRITICAL SUBSTANCES

Sugars

Syrup, fruit juice, fruits themselves, honey, and candy, are inherently sweet natural or processed sugar-containing energy foods that are enjoyed by both people and livestock. Semitropical sugar cane stalks and more temperate sugar beet roots yield both molasses and table sugar which contain 10-20% sucrose sugar. Glucose $C_6H_{12}O_6$ is the simplest sugar. Its molecule has only one double-bonded carbon-oxygen linkage.

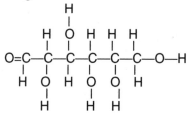

Some sugars are sweeter than others. Glucose is less sweet-tasting than sucrose. Fructose is the sweetest of the sugars. Because honey has a greater proportion of fructose than sucrose in it, honey is much sweeter than table sugar or powdered sugar. Less honey can replace any quantity of crystallized sugar to obtain the same degree of sweetness.

Sugar substitutes provide sweet taste with fewer calories. Fructose and sorbitol, which is an alcohol formed from glucose, are natural products used as substitutes. Fructose has more calories per teaspoon than sucrose, but it is so sweet-tasting that very little is needed. A potential downside of large sorbitol intake is diarrhea. Commercially manufactured (sometimes called "artificial") substitutes are saccharin, aspartame, and acesulfame-K (a potassium salt). Artificial sweeteners can cause allergic-type symptoms in some people.

Ketones

Groups attached to the carbonyl group in ketones usually contain more carbon as well as hydrogen in certain patterns. In molecules, ketones look like this,

$$\overset{\displaystyle \overset{O}{\underset{\|}{}}}{R-C-R}$$

where R is a carbon atom of another chemical group. Each R in the acetone structure symbolizes a methyl group, $-CH_3$.

Acetone C_3H_6O is the simplest ketone. Its molecule also has only one double-bonded carbon-oxygen linkage, but methyl groups flank each of the end carbons. It is a useful solvent in nail polish remover, rubber cement, paint for miniature model-making, varnishes, waxes, etc., that should never be ingested.

$$\begin{array}{ccccc} & H & & O & & H \\ & | & & \| & & | \\ H-&C&-&C&-&C&-H \\ & | & & & & | \\ & H & & & & H \end{array}$$

BODY FLUID TESTING

Screening for critical substances can be done with reagent strips ("dipsticks") or reagent tablets. *Reagents* are chemical substances that cause a very specific chemical reaction to occur in the presence of certain other substances. They serve to detect, measure, examine, or produce other substances. Reagents that change color are *chromagens*, from Greek words meaning "color producers." When their color changes indicate how much of a substance is present, they are *colormetric* or "color measurers."

Glucose can be detected in either blood or urine with the reagents glucose oxidase and peroxidase:

$$glucose + O_2 \xrightarrow{\text{glucose oxidase}} gluconic\ acid + H_2O_2$$

$$H_2O_2 + chromagen \xrightarrow{\text{peroxidase}} oxidized\ chromagen + H_2O$$
(the color change)

However, detecting sugar in blood is easier, more accurate, and less dangerous than detecting it in urine. Few health care professionals recommend urine sugar testing anymore, but you will still find test kits available in pharmacies.

Urine Testing

Urine Sugar Levels

Urine sugars are not very helpful in managing diabetes, but this is what the readings mean:
- A trace reading means the blood sugar has been above 160 mg/dl for a short time recently.
- The higher the reading, the longer and/or more severe the blood sugar high has been.

Some people spill urine sugar only when their blood sugar is very high, for example, at more than 300 mg/dl; these people have a "high sugar threshold." Although they usually have negative urine sugar tests, other tests show their diabetes is in poor control. An individual may show no urine sugar and, at the same time, have a blood sugar of 60, 120, or even 240 mg/dl. In the presence of vitamin C, when using the glucose oxidase paper test strips, it's quite possible to get a false negative for glucose.

Other people can have a "low sugar threshold," and spill urine sugar anytime their blood sugar is only 130 mg/dl. Although this may happen often, other tests could show that their diabetes is in good control. Also, dipsticks exposed to air for a week or more because, for example, they were left in an uncapped bottle, may show a false positive; you may be led to think that sugar has spilled into your urine and be very wrong. Tablets may also result in false positives.

Urine Sugar Test Strips

Strips test only for one kind of sugar, glucose. However, some urine test strips measure pH (its acidity) and specific gravity (its weight ratio to water) and detect other substances, like ketones and proteins. Each manufacturer may choose different colormetric reagents, with their own color codes to show how much urine glucose or acetone is present at the time of testing.

Urine Sugar Test Tablets

Test tablets are poison and cause severe burns. If you do buy them, you'll need some test equipment to use these tablets: a container to hold a urine sample, a test tube, and a wire clamp to hold the tube, plus a timer that registers seconds.

You should never use urine sugar test tablet results as the sole basis for adjusting insulin dosage. Tablet kits measure many sugars, not just one: glucose, fructose, lactose, galactose, pentose. Package inserts include color charts and instructions for test methods that may require one, two, or five drops of urine. These drop methods are based on Benedict's copper reduction reaction:

hot alkaline solution
$$Cu^{++} \xrightarrow{\hspace{4cm}} Cu^{+}$$

$$Cu^{+} + OH^{-} \xrightarrow{\hspace{2cm}} CuOH \text{ (yellow)}$$

heat
$$2CuOH \xrightarrow{\hspace{2cm}} Cu_2O \text{ (red)} + H_2O$$

Copper sulfate (Cu_2SO_4) reacts with the sugars in the urine, converting cupric sulfate to cuprous oxide. The reaction of sodium hydroxide with water and citric acid produces heat, which causes the contents of the test tube to boil and bubble.

BLOOD

A major purpose of blood is to carry substances from place to place inside our bodies. It whisks away waste products like carbon dioxide within body cell sites to the lungs and picks up fresh oxygen in exchange.

Plasma, the liquid portion of our blood, is 92% *water.* It is grayish yellow in color because it consists of various proteins, including *serum albumin.* Proteins, built from amino acids, include many substances, such as *hormones* (like insulin, glucagon, or adrenaline), *enzymes* (like glucose oxidase), and *antibodies* (like immunoglobulins). Blood contains all of these proteins.

Suspended in the protein plasma are *red blood cells* that transport respiratory gases, *white blood cells* that fight infections, and irregularly-shaped blood *platelets* that promote blood clotting. Each red blood cell has a life span of two to three months, with new cells to replace them produced within the bone marrow.

Hemoglobin

Abbreviated Hb, hemoglobin is the respiratory protein of red blood cells. Several forms of hemoglobin exist.

Hemoglobin A (HbA) is the form found in normal adults. When combined with inhaled oxygen, it is called oxyhemoglobin as it moves from the lungs to bodily tissues. There, as oxygen is readily released, the oxyhemoglobin reverts to hemoglobin that then picks up waste carbon dioxide from the tissues for transport back to the lungs and exhalation. Other substances can also combine with the protein HbA, for example, sugar. This results in glycohemoglobin (HbA1c). That glucose attaches to proteins may be a general factor in the process of aging since diabetes does cause early aging of blood vessels.

Glycohemoglobin (HbA1c)

A small amount of HbA1c is normal even in people who don't have diabetes. What is considered a normal percentage range, for example 4.4-6.4%, may vary according to different laboratories, their testing methods, and adopted standards. Blood sugar levels under 180 mg/dl may contain HbA1c in this range. Rarely would normal blood glucose exceed 200 mg/dl, even two hours after a meal.

HbA1c is commonly made when blood sugar levels are above 180 mg/dl. Sugar stays attached for the life of the red blood cell, about 100 days. Whether you have diabetes or not, the lower your HbA1c level is, the better off you are.

The HbA1c laboratory blood test reflects how often the blood sugars have been high for the past three months. It's a measure of the cumulated blood sugar, not the average amount, over the preceding months. HbA1c tests were developed in the 1970s, and now several different methods exist to determine glycohemoglobin. Values for desired results depend both on which method is used and on a person's age. Measured by any test method, desired ranges for teens with diabetes all fall below 10%; anything below 6% comes close to ideal.

Higher than these desired HbA1c values usually warrant increased doses of insulin. A decision to increase your dose should be thoroughly discussed with your health care provider to prevent blood sugars that are too low. High HbA1c levels are typical in smokers because smoking increases levels of hormones, like adrenaline, which raise blood sugar. Some protein loss, particularly of albumin, occurs in the urine because the kidneys have been damaged.

Poor blood glucose control, as reflected in less than normal adolescent height and weight, correlates with higher HbA1c levels. The lower this percentage of HbA1c is, the better the chance of reducing risks of long-term kidney and eye complications.

Good blood glucose control generally requires keeping blood sugar down in the hour after a meal; this means that insulin needs to be already in the body to help metabolize food when it is eaten. Nothing special a patient does on the day or two before a regularly scheduled exam can alter the results of the HbA1c test. However, if several daily blood sugar measurements are taken to check on the correct dose of insulin needed and/or if exercise is a habit that helps keep body weight in check, low HbA1c values are more than likely.

Carbos and Fats

Glycogen is more complex than the original plant starch, but readily changes to glucose as needed by the body for its energy needs. It may yield the secondary sugars maltose and dextrin before breaking down to glucose. A common test for starch involves placing a drop of iodine on an unknown substance; if a deep dark blue appears, starch is present.

Decomposition of starches involves hydrolysis reactions in which water catalyzes their conversion to the sugar glucose. The blood transports glucose from its production at digestive sites to the liver and muscle tissue where it is stored as *glycogen*, the main form of carbohydrate storage in animals. Reacting with the water in pancreatic juice, maltose converts to glucose. In the presence of yeast, some of this glucose ferments to produce ethanol, responsible for the sweet smell of baking bread. Some foods are more complex than others and take longer to enter the bloodstream as glucose. Our bodies work to maintain a more or less even level of glucose all the time.

Healthy diets have 25-30% of their calories coming from fat *vs.* typical American diets with 40-50%. No matter what our health, current recommendations are to reduce fat intake with more unsaturated than saturated fats in a 2:1 balance. Increased unsaturated and decreased saturated fat intake helps limit the body's production of cholesterol.

Cholesterol

Our bodies need the natural *blood fat*, cholesterol, for many functions, but too much of it in our bloodstream can lead to early clogging of the arteries (arteriosclerosis) in general and clogging of the coronary arteries (heart disease) in particular. We don't need to eat cholesterol for our health. Our livers make all we need. Eating a lot of food high in saturated fats and cholesterol can increase the cholesterol levels in our bloodstream.

A proper diet and exercise help keep our cholesterol in normal range. Every year or two your doctor should test your blood lipids (cholesterol, triglycerides) and explain the results and consequences to you. About 40% of diabetics have high cholesterol. Your dietitian can help you if your levels are too high.

Bodies use cholesterol to form their cell membranes and to make steroid hormones. Approximately 85% of our total blood cholesterol is made in our own liver; foods we eat provide the remaining 15%. Cholesterol is present in some amount in all normal animal tissues, but it is concentrated in the brain and spinal cord. In a person who weighs 130 lbs, less than half a pound or 0.003% is cholesterol. It and the products of its metabolism are required for growth of almost all life forms. High levels of cholesterol in the bloodstream, however, influence disease development (blockage and/or early aging) in arterial blood vessels leading from the heart.

> "[Cholesterol] and its metabolic products are required for growth of almost all life forms."

No fat dissolves in water. For fat to travel from the liver or intestine through the bloodstream to energy use or storage sites, it must form *lipoproteins* with blood proteins. Several types of lipoproteins exist with different amounts of cholesterol, triglycerides, and other biochemical groups. The density of their components varies.

High-density lipoproteins (HDL) are small, closely-packed molecules that protect inner linings of the arteries from accumulated fat deposits. Plaques, containing cholesterol, triglycerides, and low-density lipoproteins (LDL), both separate from and attach to arterial linings, to promote atherosclerosis. Chylomicrons and very low-density lipoproteins (VLDL) are relatively large low-density types.

Cholesterol and lipoprotein measurements are part of regular check-ups because of their association with cardiovascular (heart and blood vessel) disease. Changes in diet and/or taking medication can alter levels of these blood fats and, therefore, severity of cardiovascular disease. The DCCT study showed that intensive treatment of diabetes reduced the cardiovascular disease risk by 35%.

The Centers for Disease Control and Prevention (CDC) in Atlanta uses a different chemical method to measure total cholesterol levels than almost all other laboratories. However, total cholesterol can be found indirectly and roughly by simple addition of major lipoproteins:

HDL + LDL = Total Cholesterol

A normal range for cholesterol in serum is 150-250 mg/dl, but the higher end is not considered ideal. Total cholesterol measurement is less variable than lipoprotein analyses because just the number of steps needed to separate HDL from LDL introduces more opportunity for variation.

HDL

Normal body functioning and environmental conditions bearing on the sample affect lipoprotein test results much more than analytical errors. Centrifugal forces, electrophoresis, and precipitation with calcium, magnesium, or manganese ions are only some of many methods used for separating and measuring LDL and HDL.

LDL

Both LDL and HDL stain well with red or black electrophoretic dyes. LDL precipitates, leaving HDL in the overlying liquid (supernatant) above the solid LDL, which is also known as beta-lipoprotein.

Triglycerides

Another kind of natural blood fat, triglycerides, can lead to early aging of large blood vessels. They help form plaque that hardens arteries and blocks blood flow. Triglycerides become part of exceptionally low-density lipoprotein types which literally float to the top of collected plasma when left undisturbed. Their relationship to later heart disease is less clear than for cholesterol. Eating high fiber foods and getting plenty of exercise seem to lower triglyceride levels.

As compounds found naturally in our bodies, normal levels of triglycerides vary from person to person. To accurately determine a person's triglyceride level, it is necessary to fast before giving a blood sample. Because of the uncertain relationship triglycerides have to heart disease and because fasting for testing is sometimes dangerous for people with diabetes, doctors may not test for this substance in diabetics who do not have a family history of early heart attacks.

The CDC uses a multistep chemical method for triglyceride reference values, while enzyme methods are commonly used elsewhere:

$$\text{triglyceride} + 3H_2O \xrightarrow{\text{lipase}} \text{glycerol} + \text{fatty acid}$$

Remember that an -ase ending identifies enzyme words. In both chemical and enzymatic methods, it is released glycerol that is measured. Normal levels of triglyceride in serum range from 10 mg/dl to 160 mg/dl.

Serum Proteins

Albumin is a general term for many kinds of water-soluble proteins. Prealbumin can bind with thyroxine molecules; it plays a significant role in the transport and metabolism of vitamin A through the body. Because of its large size, it does not leave the plasma in the renal glomerular filtrate. The half-life of prealbumin in circulation is roughly two days, shorter than other major serum proteins. It is an early indicator of nutritional changes.

Serum albumin is the most abundant protein (up to two-thirds of total protein) in normal blood plasma and of the serum that bathes body tissues. Dips are frequent in sick people due to losses through the kidney and into the urine. This kind of loss from within blood vessels results in serious pressure changes that cause swelling in hands, wrists, feet, and ankles. Albumin serves as a carrier protein for a variety of important substances: thyroxine, penicillin, free fatty acids, calcium, magnesium, and small amino acids. Because calcium and magnesium ions bind to albumin, measurement of albumin also allows management of these nutrients.

During periods of high blood sugar, up to 25% of serum albumin may have attached sugars. The half-life of circulating albumin is approximately 17 days. Measurement of the glycosylated form may monitor diabetic control during a short interval.

Globulins are simple proteins that do not dissolve in water, so it seems odd that they should be a normal part of our blood liquid that is 92% water.

Detection of prealbumin, albumin, LDL, specific globulins, and fibrinogen involves electrophoresis and conventionally-stained gels. Prealbumin migrates faster than albumin to the positive pole in electrophoretic systems. Typical amounts in serum are 3.2-4.5 g/dl albumin and 2.3-3.4 g/dl globulins. Total proteins in serum normally range from 6.0-7.8 g/dl. Immunologic methods are used for other serum proteins that have levels too low for electrophoresis.

Thyroxine (T4)

Thyroxine is a hormone made by your thyroid gland. It is located around your voice box. Growth spurts during teenage years will not be normal if the thyroid gland is not functioning properly. That's why routine visits to your health care team include tests to monitor its size and function.

The thyroid gland produces several iodine-containing hormones that have multiple functions:
- Increase respiration
- Regulate the turnover of carbohydrates, lipids, and proteins
- Promote glucose absorption, glucose regeneration by the liver and kidney, glucose use in muscle and fat tissues
- Degrade glycogen in the liver
- Increase LDL degradation and cholesterol disposal
- Stimulate metabolic enzymes

Among them, thyroxine was first to be discovered. Because each of its molecules contains four iodine atoms, thyroxine is abbreviated as T4. Once secreted into plasma surrounding the gland's cells and then into the thyroid vein, T4 associates with the plasma proteins (albumins and globulins), which carry it to the liver and kidney for metabolism and storage. It increases the rate of cell metabolism (oxygen consumption, also an insulin function) and regulates growth (protein synthesis).

The action of thyroid hormones on LDL and cholesterol lowers their blood plasma levels. Increased oxygen demand due to too much thyroxine (hyperthyroidism or overactive thyroid gland) increases heart rate and blood output, thereby straining the heart. Exaggerated catabolism leads to decreased serum cholesterol and possibly also to poor glucose tolerance and sugar in the urine.

If the thyroid is enlarged, the nurse may recommend a thyroid-stimulating hormone (TSH) blood test. This is the first test to become abnormal when an allergic-type problem occurs. The blood carries antibodies against the diabetic's own thyroid gland, making just one more autoimmune assault to deal with. Fortunately, this condition can be treated easily with a once-a-day thyroid tablet. A small percentage of people with diabetes also have a lack of thyroxine. Simply taking a thyroid replacement pill every day takes care of this problem, too.

Laboratory methods of measuring T4 have changed in the last 50 years. Radioimmunoassays (RIA) with radioactive-labeled T4 give normal results of 5.5 µg-12.6 µg/dl. An even more specific method, which detects TSH, is used on samples from people suspected of having an overactive thyroid gland.

The more thyroxine present, the higher the basal metabolic rate (BMR). Degeneration of renal tubules may cause less protein attachment to thyroxine. This is marked by noninflammatory swelling, albuminuria, and decreased serum albumin.

URINE

Normally a slightly acid (pH4-6), clear, fluid waste material that kidneys secrete in mammals, urine is 96%

Laboratory Test Results

Component	Body Fluid	Normal Range	Ideal
albumin	serum	3-5 g/dl	4 g/dl
cholesterol	blood	150-240 mg/dl	below 200 mg/dl
globulins	serum	2-3 g/dl	2.5 g/dl
glucose (sugar)	blood	60-140 mg/dl	80-120 mg/dl
	urine	0.1-0.3 g/24 hrs	0.2 g/24 hrs
glycohemo-globin (HbA1c)	blood	4-8%	below 6%
HDLs	blood	~	above 35 mg/dl
ketones	urine	0	0
LDLs	blood	~	below 130 mg/dl
microalbu-minuria	urine	below 7 µg/min	3-4 µg/min
thyroxine (T4)	blood	6-13 µg/dl	9 µg/dl
total proteins	serum	6-8 g/dl	7 g/dl
triglycerides	serum	10-160 mg/dl	75-80 mg/dl

water and rich in end products of protein metabolism, salts, and pigments. Urine's yellow to amber color comes from the breakdown of blood protein pigments. As the chief component (2%) of urine, *urea* is the major nitrogenous end product of protein metabolism that is carried to the kidneys by blood plasma. *Uric acid* is another such end product at 0.05%. The remainder is equal portions of electrolytes (sodium, chloride, potassium, phosphate, and sulfate ions) and nonelectrolytes.

Approximately 1200 ml of blood per minute flows through small blood vessels in the kidneys. There it is filtered by kidney cells called glomeruli, and the resulting filtrate is a fluid containing substances not attached to blood plasma proteins. The glomerular filtration rate averages 125 ml/minute. As the filtrate passes through other kidney cells, significant portions of many substances (including water, glucose, amino acids, and vitamins) are reabsorbed along the way. In fact, only 2% of the water from the glomerular filtrate is excreted in the urine, concentrating other substances in it.

When blood sugar levels are high, not only is sugar excreted in the urine, but pressure increases in the glomeruli and damages the small blood vessels that bring plasma for filtration there. Some proteins start to leak through the filter and show up in the urine.

"Bad Proteins"

Proteins themselves are not bad or good. Just as weeds may be considered bad plants because they grow where we don't particularly want them, some blood proteins spill into our urine (*proteinuria* is the general term), when normally they're too large to leave the small renal arterioles and enter the glomeruli. While not bad themselves, their presence here gives bad news of potential kidney damage.

Globulins not soluble in water change their ability to dissolve in salt solutions. The sodium and chloride ions in urine provide the right environment for this change. When the globulin is present in urine, *globulin-uria* results. When albumin passes into the urine (a condition known as *albumin-uria)*, even in trace amounts, something might be wrong. Disease may affect the permeability of the kidney glomeruli, allowing plasma proteins to pass through its walls. Progression of diabetic nephropathy can be measured by the presence of albumin in the urine be-cause it tends to appear ahead of other serum proteins during renal glomerular

> "Proteins... where we don't par-ticularly want them... give bad news."

damage. However, it is also normal for healthy individuals to be albuminuric, for example, children, premenstrual and pregnant women, and anyone who exercises intensely.

Kidney damage can result from many different diseases. High glycohemoglobin levels and high blood pressure contribute to causing proteinuria. You can slow such damage by eating less protein after consulting with your dietitian. Most Americans, whether healthy or with some disease, eat much more protein than they actually need.

Microalbumin Test

To detect kidney damage from diabetes, at a stage in which it might still be reversible, the microalbumin urine test on overnight or 24-hour urine samples was not devel-oped until the 1980s. Results are given in micrograms (µg). If your results are above 30 µg/minute, you have *micro-albuminuria* which increases your risk for developing diabetic nephropathy and kidney failure to 95%.

It is important that teen diabetics get special direc-tions from their health care providers to collect urine samples. Do this test up to twice a year. Also discuss with them steps to keep the results below 30 µg/minute.

Several precipitation methods with one kind of acid or another (acetic acid, picric acid, sulfosalicylic acid) have been used in the past. The immunologic measurement of microalbumin in urine once a year has been considered standard care for management of diabetes mellitus and the early detection of diabetic complications since 1989.

A "borderline microalbumin level" is any value between 7.6 µg/minute and 30 µg/minute. To maintain this level requires good control of blood sugar and/or blood pressure. These kinds of control, plus taking special medications, may still reverse higher microalbuminuria levels, but microalbuminuria levels above 200 µg/minute characterize full-blown nephropathy or kidney disease. Anyone whose level is above 30 µg/minute should decrease the amount of protein they eat to lessen the load on their kidneys.

INSULINS

The liver is the major site of insulin metabolism (50% of the insulin that arrives in the liver is used there), with the kidney next (30-40%).

Other laboratory research in the 1990s has produced insulins with different absorption rates than injectables, such as eye drops and nasal sprays, that are still under development by pharmaceutical companies.

A natural insulin-like compound has been isolated from fungus found in the jungles of the Congo. Unlike insulin, however, it can be taken in pill form and absorbed by the digestive system and still lower animal blood sugar. Discovered at the turn of the 21st century, many years of testing in animals and humans lie ahead before this compound becomes commercially available.

Bioengineering is an innovative way of tricking non-functioning pancreatic cells into producing insulin. Scientists at the Joslin Diabetes Center already have been successful doing this in mice. While cell or organ transplants seem like obvious solutions, they incur formidable problems with the recipient's immune system. Research is ongoing for a cure for diabetes as well as better treatments.

SUPPORT ORGANIZATIONS

The table on the following page includes national and international contacts for research and education, health care, administrative support, and recreation. People of any age with diabetes can learn from each other in formal and informal networks. Make the best of what is available.

Organization	Address	Phone
American Diabetes Association	1660 Duke St. Alexandria, VA 22314	1-800-232-3472
Association for the Care of Children's Health	7910 Woodmount Ave. Suite 300 Bethesda, MD 20814	1-301-654-6549
The Barton Center for Diabetes Education	PO Box 768 North Oxford, MA 01537	1-508-987-2056
Children's Diabetes Foundation at Denver	700 Delaware St. Denver, CO 80204	1-800-695-2873
Diabetes Camping Association	46 Deaton Rd. Lacey's Springs, AL 35754	1-256-883-2556
Federation for Children with Special Needs	95 Berkeley St. Suite 104 Boston, MA 02116	1-617-482-2915
Juvenile Diabetes Foundation International	432 Park Ave. South New York, NY 10016	1-800-223-1138
MedicAlert Foundation International	2323 Colorado Ave. Turlock, CA 95381-1009	1-800-432-5378; 1-209-669-2457
National Diabetes Information Clearinghouse	Box NDC Bethesda, MD 20892	1-301-468-2162

Readings

SUPPORT INFORMATION

American Diabetes Association. "Care of children
with diabetes in the school and day care
setting." *Diabetes Care*, 22 suppl.1: 1999 Jan;
S94-S97.

American Diabetes Association. *Your school and
your rights: discrimination against children
with diabetes in the public school system.*
Alexandria, VA, 1995.

American Diabetes Association and American
Dietetic Association. *Exchange lists for meal
planning,* rev. ed. Alexandria, VA, and
Chicago, IL, 1989.

Chase, H.P. *Understanding insulin dependent diabetes,* 7th ed. Denver, CO: Children's Diabetes
Foundation at Denver, 1992.

Clark, L.M., *et al.* "Guidelines for the student with diabetes: a school policy." *Diabetes Educator,* 18(6): 1992 Nov-Dec; 515, 517, 519.

Dickinson, J.K. "Diabetes scoop: the value of balance in the lives of kids with diabetes." *The Barton Spirit:* 1999 Spring; 2.

Minnesota. State Department of Health. *Diabetes: guidelines of care for children with special health care needs.* Minneapolis, MN, 1990.

Vennum, M.K. "Students with diabetes: is there legal protection?" *Journal of Law and Education,* 24(1): 1995 Winter; 33-67.

Wentworth, S.M., and J. Hoover. "The student with diabetes." *Today's Education,* 70(1): 1981 Feb-Mar; 42-44.

Wishnietsky, D.B., and D.H. Wishnietsky. *Managing chronic illness in the classroom.* Bloomington, IN: Phi Delta Kappa Foundation, 1996.

Woodinville Medical Center Pharmacy. Education
modules. Woodinville, WA, 1999 Jan.
Internet URL, *http://www.diabetesclub.com*

MEDICAL AND SCIENTIFIC INFORMATION

American Heritage Stedman's medical dictionary.
Boston, MA: Houghton Mifflin, 1995.

Arnst, Catherine. "Diabetes: is there a cure on the
horizon?" *Business Week*, (3638): 1999 July
19; 69, 73, 75.

DeGroot, L.J., *et al. Endocrinology*, 3d ed. Philadelphia, PA: W.B. Saunders, 1995.

Diabetes Control and Complications Trial
Research Group. "The effect of intensive
treatment of diabetes on the development
and progression of long-term complications
in insulin-dependent diabetes." *New England Journal of Medicine,* 329(14): 1993
Sept 30; 977-986.

Dorland's illustrated medical dictionary, 22d and 26th eds. Philadelphia, PA: W.B. Saunders, 1951 and 1985.

Edelsein, C.L., *et al.* "Etiology, pathogenesis, and management of renal failure," Chap 8 in *Campbell's urology,* 7th ed. 2 vols. Philadelphia, PA: W.B. Saunders, 1998.

Eli Lilly & Co. Indianapolis, IN, 1999 Mar. Internet URL, *http://www.elililly.com*

Foye, W.O., T.L. Lemke, and D.A. Williams, eds. *Principles of medicinal chemistry,* 4th ed. Media, PA: Williams & Wilkins, 1995.

Henry, J.B., R.B. Lauzon, and G.B. Schumann. "Basic examination of urine," Chap 18 in *Clinical and diagnosis management by laboratory methods,* 19th ed., edited by J.B. Henry. Philadelphia, PA: W.B. Saunders, 1996.

Hoffman, M. *Yesterday is tomorrow; a personal history.* New York, NY: Crown, 1965.

Kahn, C.R., and G.C. Weir, eds. *Joslin's diabetes mellitus,* 13th ed. Philadelphia, PA: Lea & Febiger, 1994.

Merck manual of medical information, home ed. Whitehouse Station, NJ: Merck & Co., 1977.

Morgensen, C.E. "Prevention and treatment of renal disease in insulin-dependent diabetes mellitus." *Seminars in Nephrology,* 10(3): 1990 May; 260-273.

Novo Nordisk A/S. Copenhagen, Denmark, 1999 Mar. Internet URL, *http://www.novo.dk*

Palumbo, P.J. "Diabetes control and complications trial: the continuing challenge ahead," editorial. *Mayo Clinic Proceedings,* 68(11): 1993 Nov; 1126-1127.

Pfizer, Inc. *Annual report 1998.* New York, NY, 1999.

Storer, T.I. *General zoology,* 2d ed. New York, NY: McGraw-Hill, 1951.

Streitwieser, A., C.H. Heathcock, and G.M. Kosower, eds. "Carbohydrates," Chap 28 in *Introduction to organic chemistry*, 4th ed. New York, NY: Macmillan, 1992.

Thomas, P.K., and D.R. Tomlinson. "Diabetic and hypoglycemic neuropathy," Chap 64 in *Peripheral neuropathy*, 3rd ed., edited by P.J. Dyck and P.K. Thomas. Philadelphia, PA: W.B. Saunders, 1993.

Wallach, J. *Interpretation of diagnostic tests*, 6th ed. Boston, MA: Little Brown, 1996. pp. 83, 91, 869.

Young, J.B., and L. Landsburg. "Catecholamines and the adrenal medulla," Chap 13 in *Williams textbook of endocrinology*, 9th ed., edited by J.D. Wilson, *et al.* Philadelphia, PA: W.B. Saunders, 1998.

Index

Note: **Boldface page numbers** indicate definitions. *Italic page numbers* refer to photos. When the *italic letter f* or *t* follows an Arabic page number, it respectively refers to a *figure* or *table*.

abbreviations, 7*t*, 126–127, 133
abdomen, injection site, 49–50, 97
absorption, 77
  fiber and, 57–58
  meals and, 65*f*, 72
  rates, 56*t*, 80, 82, 96–98, 129, 138
  reabsorption, 136
accident prevention, 16, 71, 125
acesulfame-K, sweetener, 123
acetate buffers, 55*t*
acetone, 5, 123, 123*f*, 125
acidosis. *See* diabetic ketoacidosis
acids, 5, 18
  amino, 126, 132, 136
  fatty, 60, 132
  urine pH and, 5, 125, 134
acknowledgments, xiv–xv
activities, 40, 71, *118–119*
  blood sugar levels, viii, 29, 40, 83, 91*t*
  exercise, 38–41, 47, 77, *82*, 91*t*
  insulin, 5, 63–64, 77, 83
  See also main headings,
    athletics; exercise
adolescents. *See* teenagers with diabetes; teenagers without diabetes

adrenal glands, 90
adrenaline, 19, 31–32, 32, 83, 126, 128
adult-onset diabetes. *See* Type II diabetes
aging, blood vessels, 57, 127, 131
air, 14, 20, 21
albumin
  detection of, 70, 133, 137–138
  losses in urine, 128, 132, 134, 137–138
  as protein, 60, 132
  serum, in plasma, 126, 132–134
alcohol swabs, 14, 21, 33, 34*f*, 35
alcohols, 122*t*, 123, 129, 132
American Diabetes Association, 46–49, 68, 140*t*
Americans with Disabilities Act, 48–49
amino acids, 126, 132, 136
ammonium ions, excretion of, 5
amputation prevention, 68
amylase, enzyme, 59
amylose, polysaccharide, 59
anabolism, **31**
anatomy, emergencies and, 14
animals
  fats of, 60, 80, 129

animals, *continued*
glycogen in, 30, 59, 83, 128
sugar production, 4, 54, 123
ankles, swelling of, 132
antibodies, 126
anxiety, x, 13, 26, 29, 63
choices and, 35, 41, 82–83, 117
arms, 49–50, 68, 97
arteries, 129–131
cholesterol and, 129
arterioles, 136
aspartame, sweetener, 123
Association for the Care of Children's Health, 140*t*
atherosclerosis, plaques and, 130
athletics, 1, 46
attending, 52–53
food and, 35–36, 38–41, 72, 77
participating in, 63–64, 75–78
planning ahead for, 35–36, 76–77
attitudes
healthy, vii, 32, 35, 40, 95
troublesome, viii, x, xix

balance, **4, 32,** 68
food and, 32, 40, 56, 80
kinds of, 4, 31–32, 91*t*
overcompensation *vs.*, 26–27, 88
stress and exercise, 82–83
Banting, Sir Frederick, xiv
Barton Center for Diabetes Education, 140*t*
basal metabolic rate (BMR), **31,** 134
basketball, 1, 40–41, *63, 76f,* 76–77
bathroom use, 2, 23, 25, 47–48
beans, 56, 57, 79
Benedict's copper reduction reaction, 125–126

bioengineering, 138
biohazard, **15**
biology, metric system in, 6
blindness, 67, 70
blood, 17, 45, 49, 122*t*, 126–134
cells and, 69, 126
fats in, 57, 116, 129–132
functions, 4, 126, 128
hemoglobin in, 126–128
ketones build up in, 5, 11
proteins in, 126, 132–134
sugar in (*see* blood sugar; glycohemoglobin)
testing (*see* blood sugar tests; blood tests, non-sugar)
blood flow, 68–69, 136
blood glucose. *See* blood sugar
blood plasma, 17, 126, 131
blood pressure, 111
high, supports pro-teinuria, 69, 115, 132, 137
low, 5
blood sugar, 4–5, 38, 127
activities and levels, viii, 29, 40, 83, 91*t*
changes in levels, 19, 29, 39, 73, 76–77, 83, 100–101
fine tuning and, 100–102, 106
high levels, 3, 11–12, 18–19, 27–28, 66, 115
(*see also main heading* blood sugar, uncon-trolled)
hormones and levels, 19, 30, 54
indicator amounts, **17,** 27–29, 61, 76, 90–92, 91*t*
low levels, 19, 21, 25–26, 47, 50 (*see also* hypoglycemia)
measurement units, 6–7*t*
testing (*see* blood sugar tests)

blood sugar, *continued*
  See also glycohemoglobin
blood sugar, controlled
  as achievable goal, vii, 51,
    67–68, 88, 99
  achieving, with trial and
    error, 75–76, 79, 104
  enjoyment and, 41, 94
  as false conclusion, 125
  food and, 38, 58, 78, 80
  insulin and, 12, 61, 67
  reduced risks with, 61–62,
    67–68, 70–71
  tighter control, **61,** 71, 103–
    104, 138
blood sugar, uncontrolled,
  xiii, xix, 5, 57
  body changes and, 70, 128
  as false conclusion, 16, 125
  freedom loss and, ix–x, 47,
    51–53
  long-term complications
    and, 30, 47, 62, 67–71
  pre-meal highs, 89–92, 91*t*,
    106
  pre-meal highs and
    actions, 89*f*, 90, 92
blood sugar tests, 5, 115
  equipment and supplies
    for, 12, 14–15
  glucometers and, 39, 111
  ideal results from, 67–68,
    91*t*, 92, 100*f*, 127–
    128, 135*t*
  insulin doses and, 20, 56
  laboratory *vs.* self-admin-
    istered, 17, 115, 127
  metric units and, 7*t*, 17
  post-meal, 90, 100*f*, 100–
    103, 106, 127
  pre-meal, 89–92, 91*t*, 100*f*,
    100–101, 106
  pre-snack, 100*f*, 100–101
  at school, 45, 47–48
  self-administered, 12, 14–
    15, 17–18, 28, 31, 44–
    45, 47, 79, 107, 121
blood tests, non-sugar
  hormones, 116, 134

blood tests, non-sugar
  continued
  lipids, 116, 130–132
  serum cholesterol, 130–131
  serum proteins, 133
blood vessels, 132
  damage to, 69–70
  premature aging of, 57,
    127
  specific kinds of, 70, 129–
    130, 136
BMR (basal metabolic rate),
  31, 134
body cells, 4, 31, 83, 126–127,
  129
body fluids, 58–59, 69, 132
  See also blood; urine
body fluids testing, 14–20,
  124–126
  blood sugar levels, 17–18,
    124–125
  blood test procedures, 14–
    15
  chemistry of, 16–18, 124–
    126, 130–134, 137
  urine ketone levels, 18–20
  urine ketone test supplies,
    16, 20
  urine protein levels, 137–
    138
  urine sugar levels, 18, 124–
    125
  urine sugar test supplies,
    16, 125–126
  urine test procedures, 16,
    125, 137
body height, 111, 128
body organs, damage, 67
body tissues, 18–19, 21–22,
  127, 132
  See also scar tissue; *and*
    specific organs, e.g.,
    muscles
body weight, 20, 53, 111, 128
bonds, chemical. *See* chemical bonds
bones, 68, 126
bouncing, blood sugar, 19
brain, 5, 25, 27, 68, 129

breads, 39–40, 56t, 57–59, 79–80, 81t, 128–129
breakfast foods, 23f, 23–24, 29, 38, 93–94
breath, fruity odor, 5
breathing patterns, symptom, 5
buffers, solubility and, 55
burns, 16, 125
bus drivers, first-aid, 46
buttocks, injection sites, 49–50

cakes, decorating gels for. *See* frostings
calcium ions, nutrients, 132
calories
from carbohydrates, 58, 79, 123
energy and, 58, 76f, 76–77
food groups and, 80, 80t
unburned, 77, 105
camps, ix–x, *xvii*, 140t
candy, 29, 38, 122
capillaries, 70
carbohydrate loading, **39**–41
carbohydrates, **39,** 56t, 56–59, **58**
complex, 38, 58–59, 78–80, 128–129
long-term exercise and, 39–41, 77
as normal energy source, 11, 83
simple, 80
carbon atom
in nutrients, 39
carbon atoms, 123
double-bonded to oxygen, 5, 122f, 123f
in nutrients, 58, 59
carbonyl group, in ketones, 5, 123, 123f
"carbos." *See* carbohydrates
carrier proteins, 132–134
carrying cases, for supplies, 30, 34, 34f, 36, 45
catabolism, **31,** 134
cats, diabetes in, xiv

CDC (Centers for Disease Control and Prevention), xiii, 130, 132
cells, human (general). *See* body cells
cells, plant. *See* plants, cells of
cellulose, 39, 57–59, 59, **59,** 79
Centers for Disease Control and Prevention (CDC), xiii, 130, 132
cereals, 56t–57, 81t, 94
Chase, H. Peter, MD, 19–20
cheeses, 39, 81t, 94, 94f
chemical bonds, 5, 60, 122f, 122–123, 123f
chemical groups
carbonyl, 5, 122f, 123, 123f
esters, 60
lipoproteins and, 130
methyl, 123
chemical reactions, 5, 16, 18, 124
chemistry, 6, 14
food biochemistry, 58–60, 128
substance tests, 16–18, 124–126, 130–134, 137
word construction in, 121–122, 124
children with diabetes. *See* kids with diabetes
Children's Diabetes Foundation, 140t
chloride ions, 136
cholesterol, 129–131
arteriosclerosis and, 129–130
blood, and diet, 57, 80, 82
check-ups for, 116, 130
lipoproteins and, 130–131
thyroid hormones and, 134
total, measurements, 130–131
chromagens, **16, 124**
chronic renal failure (CRF), 69–70

chylomicrons, 130
civil rights laws, 48–49
cleanliness, 14, 21, 46
color, changes, 16–18, 20,
    124–126
colormetrics, reagents as, **16**,
    20, 124–125
coma, 5, 68
combination insulin thera-
    pies
  achieving goals with, 104
  Humalog®, Regular, and
      Ultralente®, 87*f*,
      103*f*, 103–105
  Humalog® and Regular,
      105–106
  NPH and Regular, 51–53,
      63–64, 67
  Ultralente® and Regular,
      62–67, 65*f*, 77, 85,
      85*f*, 87*f*
communication
  among health care team
      members, 46
  by health care profession-
      als, xix–xx, 83, 107,
      110–116, 124
  by parents, xix–xx, 121
  by teens with diabetes, 24–
      25, 28–31, 112–114,
      121
complex carbohydrates, 38,
    58–59, 78–80, 128–129
complications of diabetes,
    67–71
  aging blood vessels, 57,
      127
  attitudes that promote, x,
      xix
  long-term, eyes, 69–71, 88
  long-term, kidneys, 61–62,
      67, 69–70, 88, 137–
      138
  long-term, nerves, 61–62,
      67–68, 88
  poor control and, 30, 47,
      62, 67–71
  reduced risks of, 61–62,
      67–68, 70–71

complications of diabetes,
    continued
  short-term emergencies, 5,
      27–31, 90
  social, 71
confusion. *See* mental
    confusion
continuous infusion pump
    therapy, 47, 72
conversion, measurements,
    7*t*
conversion values, measure-
    ment, 7*t*
convulsions, symptom, 28
cookies, 29, 38
cortisol, 90
cottage cheese, 39, 81*t*, 94
counseling, 32
crackers, 38–39, 81*t*
creatinine, 69
CRF (chronic renal failure),
    69–70
critical substances. *See*
    ketones; sugars
cubic centimeters, conver-
    sion values, 7*t*

DCCT (Diabetes Control
    and Complications
    Trial Research Group),
    61, 67–71, 130
deciliters, conversion values,
    7*t*
decorating gels. *See* frostings
dehydration, body, 5
dextrin, 59, 128
dextrose, 29
  See also glucose
diabetes, ix–xiv, **xii**
  as chronic disease, xi, 32,
      48
  complications (*see main
      heading*, complica-
      tions of diabetes)
  costs, xiii, 5, 14–15, 20, 29
  diagnosis, vii–viii, x–xi, 9–
      10, 19, 71
  education (*see main
      heading*, education)

diabetes, *continued*
poor control of (*see* blood sugar, uncontrolled)
professional care (*see* health care providers)
research, 54, 67–68, 93, 138
statistics, xiii, 68, 69, 129
support organizations, 139, 140*t*
symptoms, xii, 3
therapies, 47, 67
Diabetes Camping Association, 140*t*
diabetes care teams. *See* health care providers, as teams
Diabetes Control and Complications Trial Research Group (DCCT), 61, 67–71, 130
diabetes educators
health care teams with, 46, 110
Ms Hare, 11–13, 25–26, *113*
roles of, 66, 83, 110, 112
when to call, 19
diabetes equipment and supplies, 33–36, 125
blood tests, 12, 14–15, 44–45
carrying cases, 30, 34, 34*f*, 36, 45
consultants, 15, 111
FDA and, problems, 107
providers, 15, 37, 37*f* (*see also* pharmacies)
diabetes insipidus, xii
diabetes management
intensive, 47, 61, 63, 65–68, 70
personalized, 9–10, 36, 45–46, 92
physical skills, 9, 12, 83
planning, 33–36
poor, xviii–xix (*see also* blood sugar, uncontrolled)
support, xx, 32

diabetes mellitus
pancreas impairment and, xii, xiv, 11
pets with, xiv
symptoms, xii, xiv, xvii, 2
types of, xii–xiii (*see also* Type I diabetes; Type II diabetes)
diabetic ketoacidosis, 5, 19–20, 47, 68
diabetic nephropathy, 69–70, 88, 137–138
diabetic neuropathy, 68, 88
diabetic retinopathy, 69–71, 88
diet
blood cholesterol and, 57, 80, 82, 129
blood sugar and, 89*f*, 90
cardiovascular disease and, 130
complex carbohydrates in, 78–80
fats in, 57, 80, 82, 94, 129
food exchange lists and, **80,** 81*t*
insulins and, 56–58
well-balanced, **56,** 79–80
dietitians
health care teams with, 46, 110
Ms Larner, 13, 94, *113*
roles of, 58, 94–95, 110–111, 129
digestion, 68, 80
fiber and, 57–58
function of, 4, 57
hints to aid, 78–79
hormones and, 4, 11, 31, 56, 138
digestive diseases, institute, 67
dipsticks. *See* test strips, blood; test strips, urine
Disabilities Education Act, 48
diseases, blood-borne, 15
diseases, chronic, xi, 32, 48, 69–70, 129–130

dizziness, 25–26, 28
doctors
    attitudes of, xix
    confidence in, xx, 10
    education and, xix, 3, 15,
        61, 114, 116, 129
    expectations of, 107, 119
    as health care providers,
        xix–xx, xviii, 15, 19,
        28*f*, 45
    health care teams with, 46,
        110, *113*
    insulin and, 23, 51, 62, 66,
        83, 104–105
    patient support and, xx,
        28*f*, 61, 110, 113
    specific kinds of, xviii, 3,
        9, 68, 70
    state agencies and, 48, 71
    tighter control and, 61, 71
    when to call, 19, 92, 107
dogs, diabetes in, xiv, 54
dosage
    glucose tablets, 29
    insulin, 20, 23, 56, 63, 66–
        67
    insulin adjustments, 73,
        92, 125, 127–128
    mistakes, 16
Draznin, Martin, MD, *113*
    diabetes management, 9–
        10, 92
    insulin regimens, 61–62
    office visits, 9–10, 13, 113–
        114, 116
drinks, 48
    hypoglycemia and, 29, 34–
        35
    snacks, 38, 76, 78
driving privileges, 71
drug stores. *See* pharmacies

e-commerce, 15, 37
education
    continuing, 117–118, 121
    diabetes and, vii, x–xi,
        xix–xx, 9–13, 48–49,
        121

education, *continued*
    family needs for, 9–10, 29–
        31, 48–49
    information and, viii, 11–
        12, 107
    by manufacturers, 15
    pattern recognition skills
        and, 92, 109
    for students with diabetes,
        24, 48, 93
eggs, 60, 81*t*
electrolytes, 56, 136
emergencies, 14, 48
    diabetic ketoacidosis as, 5,
        19
    hyperglycemia, 89*f*, 90, 91*t*
    hypoglycemia, 29–31, 36
    phone numbers, 15, 29,
        107
emergency treatments, 5,
    29–31, 89*f*, 90
emotions. *See* feelings
endocrine glands
    adrenal glands, 90
    hormone secretion by, xi–
        xii
    pituitary gland, xii
    thyroid glands, 133–134
    See also pancreas
endocrinologists, 9
end-stage renal disease, 69
energy
    abnormal sources, 5, 11, 38
    exercise and, 2, 38–40, 76*f*,
        76–77
    lack of (*see* fatigue)
    normal sources, 4, 11, 19,
        31, 38, 58
    uses for, 4, 38
enzymes, 59, 122*t*, 126
    as reagents, 18, 124–125,
        132
equipment and supplies. *See*
        diabetes equipment
        and supplies
esters, 60
ethanol, 129
exchange lists, food, **80,** 81*t*

excretion, xii
  indigestible nutrients, 57, 59, 79
  water in urine, 5, 134, 136
exercise
  albuminuria with, 137
  blood lipids and, 129, 131
  blood sugar and, 4, 38, 50, 128
  energy and, 2, 38–40
  food and, 39–41, 47, 91*t*
  insulin and, 50, 83
  stress and, 32, 82–83
  See also athletics
  experiments, 39–41, 75–76, 79, 92, 104
eyes
  check-ups, 70, 113
  diabetic neuropathy and, 68
  diabetic retinopathy and, 61–62, 67, 70–71
  other problems with, xviii, 3

faintness, 25–26, 28
families
  education and, ix, 9–10, 29–31, 47
  medical history of, xii, 131
  Melluish, 1
  planning by, 46–47, 58
fasting periods, 38, 82, 131
fatigue, 2, 9, 24, 69
fats, 39, 122*t*
  as abnormal energy source, 5, 11, 38
  in blood, 129–132
  breakdown of, 18–19, 54, 57
  fiber and, absorption time, 57–58
  insulin and, 56
  as nutrients, 56–58, 60, 80, 81*t*, 82
  types of, 60, 80, 81*t*
  unhealthy diets and, 57, 80, 94, 129
fatty acids, 60, 132

FDA (U.S. Food and Drug Administration), 104, 106–107
fear, feelings of. *See* anxiety
Federation for Children with Special Needs, 140*t*
feelings, 24, 31–32, 45, 99–100
  enjoyment, 41, 94
  See also anxiety; stress
feelings, coping with, 22, 25–26, 32, 82–83
  anxiety, 35, 41, 117
  excitement, 10, 24, 83
feet, 68, 132
Feinberg, Arthur, MD, 3, 11
fiber, 56–59, 59, 131
fine tuning, 93–106
  blood sugar levels, 100–102, 106
  injection sites, 95–97
  insulin combinations, 103–105
  nutrition, 93–95
fingers, "milking," 14
first-aid, 30, 46
fish, 81*t*, 82
Florida, liability immunity, 49
flushed feelings, 25–26
food
  biochemistry of, 58–60, 128–129
  blood sugar levels and, 4, 26
  dietitians as, consultants, 94–95, 110–111
  digestion and, 11, 31, 56, 80
  indigestion and, 78–79
  insulin and, 23, 63
  as normal energy source, 31, 38
  nutrient groups in, 11, **56–**60
  planning for, 23–24, 34–36, 38–41, 47, 64, 91*t*
  stress and eating habits, 32
  sugar tests for, 16

food, *continued*
  sugars in, 4, 29, 38, 56*t*,
    56–58, 76, 78, 89*f*, 90,
    122–123
Food, Drug, and Cosmetic
  Act, 106
foot care, 68, 83
freedom
  loss of, ix, 47, 51–53
  regaining, viii–ix, xv, 45–
    46, 53, 63–67, 72–73,
    117–120
friends, 24, 29–31, 40, 52–53,
  63–64
fright, feelings of. *See*
  anxiety
frostings, 30, 35
fructose, 4, 5, 58, 123, 125–
  126
fruit juice, 29, 38–39, 46, 58,
  122
fruits, 5, 29
  components of, 38, 56*t*,
    57–58, 60, 122
  as food group, 80, 81*t*

galactose, 4, 58, 59, 125–126
galactosides, 59, 79
gallons, conversion values,
  7*t*
globulins, 126, 133–134, 136–
  137
globulinuria, 137
glomeruli, 69, 132, 136, 137
glucagon, 13, 19, 30–31, 126
glucometers. *See* glucose
  meters
glucose
  chemistry, 30, 59, 122, 122*f*,
    124
  in plasma *vs.* whole blood,
    17 (*see also* blood
    sugar *and all main
    headings following it
    which begin with*
    blood sugar)
  properties, 123, 127, 132
  sources, 4, 29, 30

glucose, *continued*
  tablets, 25–26, 29, 34–35,
    47
  in urine (*see* glucosuria)
glucose control. *See* blood
  sugar, controlled
glucose meters
  blood sugar numbers and,
    39, 100*f*, 100–102
  oversight of, 107, 111
  school life and, 33, 34*f*, 35
  self-administered blood
    tests with, 12, 14,
    17–18, 45, 107
  styles, 15, 17, 100*f*
glucose oxidase, 18, 124–126
glucose tolerance tests, 5
glucosuria, **18**, 30, 126, 136
  hormones and, 32, 134
  misleading test results, 16,
    124–125
glycerol, 132
glycogen, 30, 47, 59, 83, 128
glycohemoglobin (HbA1c),
  67–68, 115, **115,** 127–
  128, 137
grains, 56*t*, 57–59, 79
grams, conversion values, 7*t*
Greek language, English
  words from, 59, 121–
  122, 124
growth
  cholesterol required for,
    129–130
  hormones and, 20–21, 133
  as protein synthesis, 134
gut aches, sports and, 36, 78

habits, 32, 35, 97, 128
hands, 14, 28, 46, 132
Hare, Karyl, diabetes
  educator, 11–13, 25–26,
  113
HbA1c (glycohemoglobin),
  67–68, **115,** 127–128,
  137
HDL (high-density lipoproteins), 116, 130–131
head sweats, 25–26

headache, 24
health, 100, 110, 115
  diet and, 56–58, 80, 94
health care providers, xix,
  14, 30
  dietitians, 13, 46, 94–95,
    110–111, 129
  nurses, 15, 46–48, 110–111,
    114–116, 134
  objective help from, 3, 15–
    16, 124
  roles of, 127–128, 137
  as teams, xx, **46,** 92, 110,
    118, 133
  See also diabetes educa-
    tors; doctors
heart disease, 129–131
heat energy, 31
hemoglobin
  red blood cells and, 126–
    127
  sugared, blood test, 67–68,
    115, 127–128
high-density lipoproteins
  (HDL), 116, 130–131
honey, 58, 122, 123
hormones, 70, 126
  digestion and, 4, 56, 138
  insulin as, xiv, 54, 59
  secretion of, xi–xii
  specific kinds of, xiv, 19–
    21, 30, 116, 133
hospital supply companies,
  15
hospitalizations, 5, 9, 10, 19
Humalog® insulin, 86–89,
  102
  in combination, 87*f*, 103*f*,
    103–106
  freedom and, 86, 88
  mixing, in syringe, 21, 55,
    103
  snacks unnecessary with,
    87*f*, 87–88, 95
  very short action, 54*t*–55*t*,
    86, 87*f*, 89
humulin insulins, 55, 55*t*
hunger, symptom, 28
hydrogen atoms, 39, 59–60,
  123

hydrogen ions, release, 5
hyperglycemia, 47, **47,** 70,
  73*f*, 88–91
  as short-term emergency,
    89*f*, 90, 91*t*
hyperthyroidism, 134
hypoglycemia, **27,** 27–31, 68,
  71, 111–112
  anxiety about, 13, 26, 29
  combating, 28–31, 47
  communication about, 25,
    28–31, 46–47
  insulin and, 16, 27, 67
  prevention, 27–29, 46–47,
    64, 73, 73*f*, 127–128
  self-help, 28–29, 34, 36
  symptoms, 27–28, 47

ice cream, 38
identification tags. *See*
  Medical Alert identifi-
  ers
immune systems, 134, 138
immunoglobulins, 126
Individualized Health Plans,
  47
information, diabetes, viii–
  xi, xix–xx, 24–25, 44–
  45
injection sites, 45, 45*f*, 49–50
  in fine tuning, 95–97
  map, 96*f*
  overuse, 91*t*, 96–97
  rotation, 21, 95–97
insulin, 5, 54–58, 83, 126
  basal activity, 40, 64, 66,
    72, 73*f*, 92
  blood sugar levels and, 4,
    29, 37–38
  diet and, 56–58, 63
  dosage, 20, 23, 56, 63, 66–
    67, 92
  dosage adjustment, 62–67,
    73, 77, 83, 92, 125,
    127–128
  functions, 19, 54, 57–58
  as hormone, xiv, 4, 11, 12,
    54
  intermediate-acting, 54*t*–
    55*t*, 105*f*

insulin, *continued*
  long-acting, 21, 29, 54*t*–
    55*t*, 72–73, 92, 105*f*
    (*see also* specifics,
    e.g., NPH insulin;
    Lente® insulin;
    Ultralente® insulin)
  as medication, xiii, 11–12,
    20, 51, 54–56, 55*t*
  mixing, in syringe, 21, 55–
    56, 103
  overdoses, 16, 27
  physical forms, 55*t*, 138
  school life and, 34*f*, 35
  short-acting, 21, 54*t*–55*t*,
    72, 90, 105*f* (*see also*
    specifics, *e.g.*,
    Humalog® insulin;
    Regular insulin)
  temperature limits, 31, 56,
    91*t*
  therapies, 47, 51–53, 62–68,
    70, 72, 77, 85, 103–
    106
insulin combinations. *See*
  combination insulin
  therapies
insulin injections
  body sites for (*see* injection
    sites)
  do-it-yourself, 12, 21–22
  friends and, interruptions,
    52–53
  multiple, as intensive
    treatment, 47, 61, 63,
    65*f*, 65–66
  at school, 44–45, 47–49, 64
  sports activities and, 77
  timing, 23, 47, 52–53, 64–
    67, 86–88
  timing graphs, 65*f*, 71*f*, 73*f*,
    85*f*, 87*f*, 103*f*
  unobtrusive, in public, 22,
    44*f*, 44–45
  urine ketone checks and,
    19
insulin reactions. *See* hypoglycemia
insulin-dependent diabetes

  mellitus. *See* Type I
    diabetes
intensive insulin therapy, 47,
  65–68, 70
  cardiovascular risk, 130
  multiple injections, 61, 63,
    65*f*, 65–66
Internet, 37*f*, 107
intestines, 57–59
iodine atoms, thyroxine and,
  133

Johns Hopkins Hospital, 46–
  47
Joslin Diabetes Center, xiv,
  138
Juvenile Diabetes Founda-
  tion, 48–49, 140*t*
juvenile-onset diabetes. *See*
  Type I diabetes

ketoacidosis. *See* diabetic
  ketoacidosis
ketone bodies, 5
ketones, 5, 11, 123, 123*f*
  in urine (*see* ketonuria)
ketonuria, 18–20, 38, 83
  cause, 18–19
  high blood sugar and, 5,
    11, 19
  tests, 16, 18–20, 90, 125
kidneys
  blood flow through, 136
  cells of, 69, 132, 136–137
  damage to, 4, 128, 134, 137
  diseases, 61–62, 67, 69–70
  functions, 5, 69, 82, 136
  insulin metabolism in, 138
kids with diabetes
  attitudes, x, xix, 32
  blood glucose in, ix–x, 5
  education and, xiii, 48
  See also teenagers with
    diabetes
kilograms, conversion
  values, 7*t*
kits, testing, 15–16, 124
laboratory tests, 135*t*
  blood, 17, 115, 127, 130–
    134

laboratory tests, *continued*
  urine, 3, 69, 137–138
lactose, 4, 58, 125–126
lancets, 14–15, *15f*
  school life and, 33, *34f*, 35, 45
lancing devices, 14–15
Landers, Ann, columns, 22
Larner, Susan, dietitian, 13, 94, *113*
laser treatments, retinal detachment prevention, 70
Latin language, English words from, 121
laws and legislation, 48, 49, 71, 106
LDL (low-density lipoproteins), 116, 130–131, 133–134
legs, 49, 68
legumes, nutrients in, 57, 79
lente insulins, 55, 55*t*
Lente® insulin, 21, 54*t*–55*t*, 55, 105*f*
life-styles, ix–x, 117–120, *118–119*
light-headedness, 25–26, 28
lipase, enzyme, 132
lipids. *See* fats
lipodystrophies, 97
lipoproteins, 116, 130–131, 133–134
liters, conversion values, 7*t*
liver
  cholesterol production, 57, 129
  glucose and, 30, 128
  insulin and, 54, 138
logbooks, 33, 34*f*, 35
low-density lipoproteins (LDL), 116, 130–131, 133
lungs, 5, 113, 126–127

magnesium ions, as nutrients, 132
maltose, 128

mass, measurement systems, 6–7*t*
McCarthy, Michael, nurse, 111, *113*
meal planning, 32, 47, 58, 72
  attention to, 23–24, 66, 112
measurement systems, 6–7*t*
meats, 39, 76, 76*f*, 80, 81*t*
Medical Alert identifiers, 28, 28*f*, 31
medical insurance, 32
medical research, xiii–xiv, 54–56, 55*t*, 93, 138
MedicAlert Foundation International, 140*t*
medications
  diabetes, xiii, 11–12, 20, 51, 54–56, 55*t*
  for other conditions, 70, 130, 134
  oversight by FDA, 107
medicine, applied science, xiv, 6, 121–122, 138
Melluish family, *1*
mental confusion, viii, 25–26, 28
metabolism, **31**, 133–134
  abnormal, 5, 19, 69
  BMR, **31**, 134
  food and, 58, 80
  insulin, 58, 138
  normal, 27
methyl group, formula, 123
microalbuminuria, 70, 137–138
micrograms, conversion values, 7*t*
microunits, conversion values, 7*t*
milk, 39, 56*t*, 57–58, 80, 81*t*
"milking" procedure, blood testing, 14
milligrams, conversion values, 7*t*
milliliters, conversion values, 7*t*
minerals, as nutrients, 56, 132

Minnesota. Dept. of Public
    Safety, 71
moderation, **4,** 82
moisture, exposure to, 18, 20
molecules, 58–60, 122*f*, 122–
    123, 123*f*
monounsaturated fats, 60
muscles, 113
    carbohydrates stored in,
        39, 54, 128
    proteins and, 60, 82

National Diabetes Informa-
    tion Clearinghouse,
    140*t*
National Institute of Diabe-
    tes and Digestive and
    Kidney Diseases, 67
nausea, 69
needles, 15, 21–22
nephropathy. *See* diabetic
    nephropathy
nerves, 14, 22, 28, 61–62, 67–
    68
nervousness. *See* anxiety
neutral protamine
    Hagedorn. *See* NPH
    insulin
*New England Journal of
    Medicine,* on tighter
    control, 61–62, 67, 71
nighttime
    bathroom use, 2, 23
    bedtime snacks, 38, 82, 90
    overnight fasting, 38, 82
    sleep, 52, 66, 69
nitrogen atoms, 5, 59, 69, 136
Nobel Prize for Medicine,
    xiv
non-insulin-dependent
    diabetes mellitus. *See*
    Type II diabetes
NPH insulin, **55t**
    changed regimen from,
        62–63, 67
    eating schedule, 51–53
    intermediate action, 54*t*–
        55*t*

NPH insulin, *continued*
    mixing, in syringe, 21
    timing, 72–73, 73*f*
numbness, nerves and, 61–
    62, 68
nurses
    health care teams with,
        46–47, 100
    Mr McCarthy, 111, *113*
    roles for, 15, 48, 110–111,
        114–116, 134
nutrients, **56**–60
    biochemistry of, 58–60,
        128–129
    electrolytes, 56, 136
    fibers, 56–59
    minerals, 56, 132
    recommendations for, 57,
        78*f*, 79, 94–95, 110–
        111
    vitamins, 56, 125, 132, 136
    See also fats; proteins;
        starches; sugars
nutrition, as fine tuning, 93–
    95
nuts, 60, 81*t*, 82

odors, 5, 128–129
office visits
    body fluid tests, 114–116,
        133
    with doctors, 3, 9–10, 13,
        70, 110, 113–114, 116
    insulin regulation and, 83
    personnel to consult
        during, 110–114
    preparation for, 94–95,
        109–110, 116
    purposes, 110, 116
ophthalmologists, xviii, 3
ounces, conversion values,
    7*t*
overcompensation, 26–27, 88
overdoses, 16, 27
overprotection, school
    policies, 44, 47
oxygen atoms
    demand for, 31, 134

oxygen atoms, *continued*
  double-bonded to carbon
      atoms, 5, 122, 122*f*,
      123, 123*f*
  in nutrients, 39, 59, 122,
      122*f*
oxyhemoglobin, 127

pain, 21–22, 24, 36, 40, 68
pancreas
  basal insulin production,
      72
  digestive enzyme produc-
      tion, 59
  glucagon production, 30
  impairment, xii, xiv, 11,
      121, 138
  insulin extracts, xiv, 54
  learning to think like a, 63,
      101, 121
panic, feelings of. *See*
      anxiety
parents, 45, 107
  advocacy, xx, 44, 47–49
  attitudes, xix, 10, 32, 118
  civil rights and, 48–49
  education, 61–62
  understanding their
      child's diabetes, ix–
      x, 9, 12–13, 48
pastries, 29, 56*t*, 57–59
pattern recognition skills, 5,
      92, 109
peanut butter, 23*f*, 41, 80,
      81*t*, 93–94
pediatric care, 3, 9–10
pediatricians, 3, 9
penicillin, 132
Penlet®, 14, 33, 34*f*, 35
pens, record keeping and,
      33, 34*f*, 35
pentose, 125–126
peroxidase, 18, 124
peroxide, 18
pharmaceutical companies
  FDA and, 104, 106
  insulin manufacturers, 12,
      56, 104
  insulin research, 54, 138

pharmacies
  coupons and rebates from,
      15
  as free foot-screening sites,
      68
  as suppliers, 12, 16, 30, 36,
      124
phosphate buffers, 55, 55*t*
physical check-ups, 69, 129
  doctors and, xviii, 3, 70,
      110, 113, 116
  nurses and, 110–111, 114–
      116, 134
physical skills, diabetes
      management, 9, 12
physiology, emergencies
      and, 14
pints, conversion values, 7*t*
pituitary gland, impairment,
      xii
planning
  exercise, 38–41, 47, 83, 91*t*
  food, 23–24, 38–41, 47, 64,
      91*t*
  safety, 25, 28–31, 46–47, 82
  school life, 33–36, 47–49
plants, 57–60, 138
  cells of, 59–60
  nutrients in, 57–60, 80, 81*t*
  sugar production, 4, 122
plaques, lipids and, 130–131
platelets, blood, 126
podiatrists, foot screening,
      68
polysaccharides, **59**
polyunsaturated fats, 60, 82
potatoes, 56, 79
pounds, conversion values,
      7*t*
prealbumin, 132–133
preventives, 5, 67–68, 70–71,
      92
  communication, 28–30,
      46–47
  self-care, 17, 19–20, 25, 27–
      29, 64
  See also blood sugar,
      controlled; physical
      check-ups; planning

privacy guidelines, 46
Prospective Diabetes Study,
    United Kingdom, 68
protamine insulins, 55*t*, 72
proteins, 38–41, 56–60, 122*t*,
    130–134
    abnormal metabolism and,
        5, 69
    in blood, 126, 130–134,
        135*t*
    dietary, 38, 39, 41, 56–60,
        80, 82, 137–138
    experiments with, 40–41
    insulin and, 54, 56, 59
    molecular structure of, 59
proteinuria, 136–138
    albuminuria, 128, 132, 134,
        137
    contributing factors, 115,
        137
    diabetic nephropathy and,
        69–70
    globulinuria, 137
    microalbuminuria, 137–
        138
    tests, 115, 125
pulse, 5, 111
pump therapy, 47, 72
PZI insulin, 55*t*, **55t**

quarts, conversion values, 7*t*

rapid falls, blood sugar, 27,
    29
reactions, insulin. *See*
    hypoglycemia
reagents, **16,** 18, 20, **124**–126,
    132
rebates, glucose meters, 15
rebounding, blood sugar, 19
record keeping, 33, 34*f*, 35,
    39
red blood cells, 126–127
refrigeration, 18, 30–31, 36,
    38
regimens, xiii, 62–67, 77,
    104–105
Regular insulin, 77, 102

Regular insulin, *continued*
    changed regimen with, in
        combination, 62–67, 65*f*,
        85–87, 87*f*
    eating schedule, 51–53,
        86–87, 87*f*
    mixing, in syringe, 21, 55,
        103
    short action, 54*t*–55*t*
    timing, 71*f*, 71–72, 73*f*, 85*f*,
        87*f*, 103*f*
Rehabilitation Act, 48–49
renal insufficiency, 70
responsibilities, 45, 63–67
rest, 29, 31
retinal detachment, preven-
    tion, 70
retinopathy. *See* diabetic
    retinopathy
risk reduction, 61–62, 67–68,
    70–71, 128, 130

saccharine, sweetener, 123
safety planning, 71, 107
    attention to, 28–31, 46–47,
        82
    teachers and, 24–25, 29–31,
        44–47, 121
saliva, 58–59
sandwiches, 39–40, 76, 76*f*,
    80
saturated fats, **60,** 80, 81*t*,
    129
scar tissue, 70, 96–97
scared, being. *See* anxiety,
    feelings of
schedules
    eating, 51–53, *53,* 72
    school classes, 47, 63–64,
        105
    sleep, 52
school life, 33–36, 43–49
    activities, 63–64
    bathroom use, 25, 47
    civil rights impact on, 48–
        49
    classes, 43–44, 64, 105
    coping with feelings, 25–26

school life, *continued*
  health care teams and, 46–47
  medication policies, 44, 47–49
  medication policy negotiation, 44–46
  newly diagnosed patients and, 10
  planning for, 33–36, 47–49
school staff
  diabetes training for, 48–49, 121
  information plan for, 47
  liability, 49
  roles, 46–49
science, metric system in, 6
seeds, fats in, 60
self-care, diabetes management, 36, 39–41, 45–46, 101–102, 118–119, 121
semilente insulins, 55, 55*t*
serum albumin, as plasma protein, 126, 133
sexuality, stress and, 32
shakiness, 28
Sharps containers, 15, 15*f*, 22, 46
shelf-life, test strips, 18, 20
shocks, insulin. *See* hypoglycemia
sicknesses, 38
  blood components and, 90, 91*f*, 92, 132
  urine components and, 20, 38, 132
skin, 14, 21–22, 22, 69, 97
sleep, 2, 23, 52, 66, 69
sluggishness, food and, 40
smoking, HbA1c levels and, 128
snacks, 34–39, **37**
  excessive, and pre-meal highs, 90, 91*f*
  hearty, 36, 39, 76, 76*f*, 86
  hypoglycemia and, 29, 64
  school life and, 34–35, 44, 47–48
  transportable, 34–**36**, 38

snacks, *continued*
  as unnecessary, 87*f*, 87–88, 95
soda pop, 29
sodium ions, 136
sorbitol, 68, 123
spaced-out feelings, 25–26, 28
specific gravity, **125**
spinal cord, cholesterol in, 129
sports. *See* athletics
starches
  as carbohydrates, 31–32, 39–40, 57–59, 128
  complex, 38, 57–59, 80, 128
  experiments with, 40, 77
  as food group, 80, 80*t*
  in sandwiches, 76, 76*f*
  test for, 128
  USDA recommendations, 78*f*, 79
steroids, 90, 129
stomach
  abdominal injection sites, 49–50, 96*f*, 97
  fiber and food time in, 57
  gut aches, 36, 78
  gut-ache prevention, 78–79
stress, 4, 30–32, 82–83, 90, 91*f*, 105
sucrose, 4, 58, 122–123
sugar substitutes, 123
sugars, 16–19, 56–59, 122*f*, 124–126
  absorption time with fiber, 57–58
  in blood (*see* blood sugar; glycohemoglobin)
  carbohydrates and, 39, 41
  complex, 59, 79, 128
  in foods, 29, 38, 56*t*, 56–58, 78, 122–123
  as normal energy source, 19, 30, 54
  simple, 4, 11, 56*t*, 57–59, 79, 89*f*, 90, 122

sugars, *continued*
  specific kinds of, 4, 29, 58,
      122–123, 125, 128
  as starches, 31–32, 59, 79,
      128
  tests for, 16–18, 124–126
      (*see also* blood sugar
      tests)
  in urine (*see* glucosuria)
survival, learning for, 10–13,
    36
sweatiness, coping with, 25–
    26
sweetness, 122–123
swelling, 68, 132, 134
symptoms, allergic-type,
    123, 134
symptoms, chronic renal
    failure, 69
symptoms, diabetes melli-
    tus, xii, xvii–xviii, 2–3,
    9, 12, 70
  control of, xiv
symptoms, diabetic ketoaci-
    dosis, 5
symptoms, diabetic neur-
    opathy, 68
symptoms, hypoglycemia,
    27–28, 47
synthetic insulins, 55, 55*t*
syringes, 30
  insulin draws with, 12, 55–
    56
  needles on, 15, 21–22
  school life and, 33, 34*f*, 35,
    45
  use, 21–22, 45

T4 (thyroxine), 116, 132–134
table sugar, 58, 122–123
tablets
  glucose ingestible, 25–26,
    29, 34–35
  reagents in test, 16, 20,
    124–126
  urine sugar test, 124–125
tattoos, strange, 22
teachers
  communicating with, 24–

teachers
  communicating with,
      continued
        25, 29–31, 44–47, 121
  health care teams with, 46
  liability of, 49
teenagers with diabetes, *167*
  anxiety in, x, 13, 26, 29, 35
  attitudes, xix, 32, 117, 120,
      167
  blood sugar, 5, 47, 127
  diagnosed recently, vii–
      viii, x–xi, xiii, 9–10,
      19
  diagnosed years ago, ix, xi
  diet, 38, 56, 80, 82
  education, 24, 46–48, 93,
      117–118
  hormones, 20–21, 134
  lessons in self-care, 36, 39–
      41, 45–46, 63–64, 65*f*,
      66–67, 101–102, 118–
      119, 121
  life-style, *82*, 117–120, *118–
      119*
  Medical Alert identifiers,
      28, 28*f*, 31
  overprotection of, 44, 47
  physical condition, xii,
      xvii–xviii, 52, 53, 128
  planning by, 24–25, 28*f*,
      28–31, 46–47, 82
  responsibilities, 45, 63–67,
      99–100
  stress, 32, 82–83, 131
  support organizations,
      139, 140*t*
teenagers without diabetes
  diet, 38, 56, 80
  life-style, ix
  physical condition, xii, 4–
      5, 106, 127, 137
  responsibilities, 45
  stress, 32, 82–83
telephone hotlines, 15, 28*f*,
    29, 31, 107
temperature limits
  blood test strips, 18, 31
  injectables, 31, 56, 91*t*

tennis, 35–36, 50, 64
test results
  misleading, 16, 18, 124–125
  positive, 19–20
test strips, 33, 34*f*, 35, 107
test strips, blood, 14, 17–18, 31, 124
test strips, urine, 12, 16, 20, 70, 124–125
thinking ahead. *See* planning
thinking like a pancreas, 63, 101, 121
thirst, 18
thirst, excessive, xii, 2
thresholds, high *vs.* low, 124–125
thyroid gland, 133–134
thyroid-stimulating hormone (TSH), 134
thyroxine (T4), 116, 132–134
tighter control. *See* blood sugar, controlled
timing
  blood test strips, 14
  food, 35, 47, 64, 80
  food intake, 23, 52–53, 64–67, 65*f*, 86–88, 87*f*
  glucometer checks, 39, 47
  injections, 21–22, 47, 97
  insulin, 52, 55, 71*f*, 71–73, 73*f*
  urine test strips, 14, 20
tingling sensations, 28
travel preparations, 31, 46–47
trial and error, blood sugar control, 75–76, 79, 104
triglycerides, 130, 132
TSH (thyroid-stimulating hormone), 134
Type I diabetes, 69
  history, xiii
  Medical Alert tags, 28, 28*f*, 31
  New England Journal of Medicine, 61–62, 67
  in perspective, vii, xv
  statistics, xii–xiii

Type I diabetes, *continued*
  See also diabetes *and all main headings following it which begin with* diabetes *or* diabetic, *except* diabetes insipidus
Type II diabetes, xii

Ultralente® insulin, 77
  changed regimen with, 62–67, 65*f*, 85, 85*f*, 87*f*
  long action of, 54*t*–55*t*
  mixing, in syringe, 21, 55, 65, 103
unconsciousness, 5, 13, 19, 68
  help from others, 29–31
  hypoglycemia and, 28, 71
  Medical Alert tags and, 28, 31
units (adopted standard quantity), abbreviation, 7*t*
unsaturated fats, **60,** 80, 81*t*
urea, 69, 136
uric acid, 136
urinalyses, laboratory, 3, 69
urination, xii, 2–3, 18, 23
urine
  normal expectations, xii, 69, 134–136, 135*t*, 136
  pH, 5, 125, 134
  See also glucosuria; ketonuria; proteinuria
urine tests
  check-ups, 5, 111, 115
  ideal results, 135*t*
  not recommended for glucose, 16, 18, 124–125
  self-administered, 12, 16, 19–20, 90, 124–126
  See also urinalyses, laboratory
U.S. Dept. of Agriculture, 57, 78*f*, 79

U.S. Dept. of Health and Human Services, 106
U.S. Food and Drug Administration, 104, 106–107
USDA (U.S. Dept. of Agriculture), nutrient recommendations, 57, 78*f*, 79

Van Buren Youth Camp, *xvii*, *118–119*
vegetables, 56*t*, 57–59, 60, 79–80, 80, 81*t*
very low-density lipoproteins (VLDL), 130–131
virtual stores, 37, 37*f*
vision, xviii, 3, 62, 67–68, 70
vitamins, 56, 136
  vitamin A, 132
  vitamin C, 125
VLDL (very low-density lipoproteins), 130–131
volume, measurement systems, 6–7*t*
vomiting, 69

warnings
  abnormal metabolism, 19
  biohazards, 15, *15f*, 21

warnings, *continued*
  danger, 16, 125, 131
  hypoglycemia, 17
  insulin, 55–56, 125
  overcompensation, 26–27, 88
  syringes, 21, 55–56
  wastes, blood, 45, 69, 126–127, 136
water
  needs for, xii, 48
  in urine, 5, 134, 136
weakness, 28
weight, human. *See* body weight
weight resistance, muscles and, 82
weights and measures, systems, 6–7*t*
white blood cells, 126
worry. *See* anxiety, feelings of
wrists, swelling, 132

young adults with diabetes. *See* teenagers with diabetes

zinc insulins, 55*t*

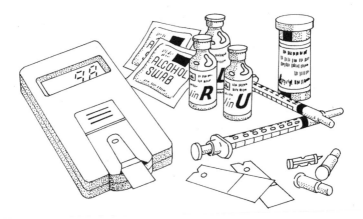

About the Author

Bill Melluish lives life impulsively and has since he was a child. He has been an unpredictable son, brother, and friend. Friendship has always been an essential part of his life in sports, extracurricular activities, and various organizations. Keeping his body in a state of good health was the last thing on his mind—as long as he could make the next game or next meeting.  After his diagnosis of juvenile diabetes, he felt forced to stay close to home, while his friends were out experiencing new things.

He won back lost freedom by combining the steps discussed in this book with hard work and determination. Now his life is mostly without worry. His high energy level and busy schedule are back, having chosen an out-of-state college. Bill is a student at Pennsylvania State University.

Flower Press is committed to creating
publications designed to help people
regain control over their own lives. By
developing skills, sharing knowledge,
and working cooperatively,
we can accomplish
together what none
of us could do alone.

Flower
Press